JONATHAN FIRTH

How to Learn

Effective study and revision methods for any course

Contents

About the author

Jonathan Firth is an author, researcher, psychology teacher and teacher trainer. He writes books and resources for both students and teachers, including psychology textbooks for high school level. His most recent publications include *Psychology in the Classroom* (2018, published by Routledge), and *AQA GCSE Psychology Revision and Practice* (2017, published by Collins). Jonathan tweets at @JW_Firth and you can find out more about his latest publications via jonathanfirth.co.uk/books

Jonathan has been a teacher for over 20 years. Having spent many years working at high school level, he now teaches at the University of Strathclyde, Glasgow, Scotland. His research focuses on memory, learning, and metacognition.

Preface

I have been studying and researching the psychology of learning and memory since the 1990s. One thing that I noticed early was that even when people have learned certain facts about human memory and study skills, they fail to put these into practice the majority of the time. The more pressure they are under, the more they seem to revert to techniques which are flawed and ineffective.

To some extent this makes sense on the basis of experience and habits. As children, we learn to prepare for simple school tests the night before, and usually manage to pass the next day. This experience teaches a very powerful message—last minute cramming works. The trouble is, such a strategy is tried and tested at the age of 12 or 13, but is simply inappropriate for the volume of material and depth of understanding needed for exam-based courses.

It's also clear that many guides to revision, while well intentioned, don't really tackle the key issues of learning, and instead focus on how to manage stress at exam time, with vague advice such as 'keep hydrated', and even neuro-myths such as 'find your learning style'. My aim in writing this book is to share some of my scientific know-how in learning and memory with you, and to provide an easy-to-read book that tackles flawed learning strategies and gives a clear, evidence-based alternative that you can put into practice right away.

Unlike many study guides, this book is not full of pseudo-science, it doesn't just focus on relaxation (taking a herbal bath might be pleasant, but that's not enough to get you through your exam!) and it DOES focus on how to understand and remember more, better and for longer.

1

Introduction

S tudy can be hard work, and yet sometimes you feel as if you are hardly making any progress. For all your effort, note-taking and time in class, you still don't really understand and remember the key information.

This can be due to the techniques and choices you make during learning and revision. You can expend a lot of effort with very little payoff if your technique is wrong. Picture a swimming pool—some people seem to glide through the water almost effortlessly, while others splash around and cover very little distance before they get tired or need a break. This is a good analogy for how different students prepare for exams.

As with so many things (diet, exercise, and so on...), it's not so much *how much* you study, as *how well* you study. The trouble is, most people don't actually know how to study—we have developed a set of assumptions and habits, or copied the habits of others. Perhaps parents have told us 'study hard' or friends have given us advice on what worked for them.

As you will see throughout this book, many of these assumptions and habits are flawed. Learners—even successful ones—often have little insight into why they are learning well, and may give advice that is unhelpful or even counterproductive. Teachers, too, for all their subject-specific expertise, often lack the psychological know-how to guide students in using their memory optimally. This is because many teachers lack a science-based understanding of how memory works (although fortunately this seems to be changing in recent years!), and therefore recommend strategies that are either flawed, or which tackle only part of the problem. For example, teachers often place a big emphasis on repetition, when (as we will see), several other factors play a bigger role in developing the memories, skills and understanding needed to get that top grade.

Changing times

In addition, the demands of study and revision change over time, meaning that study strategies will also need to change. Most people maintain the same study habits over a number of years—perhaps you are still using the same strategies that you used in the early years of high school. But are these strategies actually effective?

To take an analogy, imagine that a surgeon or dentist is still using the same techniques that she learned in the first few months of university. She wants to be effective for her patients, but is held back by using over-simplistic, ineffective skills. The same would hold for a chef or a mechanic. It doesn't really make sense, does it? If you want to get a better result, you need to improve your technique. But most people fail to apply this to studying, in part because (as mentioned above) they tend to be unaware of what the most effective learning techniques are.

So where can we get better ideas from? One key source

is the science of learning. This is a growing field, drawing on years of work by researchers from a range of disciplines including cognitive psychology, neuroscience, and education. Researchers have actually been studying learning for over a hundred years, but in the last couple of decades computer-based experimentation and other technology, combined with advances in neuroscience, have seen a real leap forward in how well scientists understand how learning works. This understanding is increasingly being applied to school and university contexts.

Can I really improve how I learn?

The simple answer is yes, you can improve the way you study. It's important to see learning as a skill—a complex one. As with another skill such as cooking, you can continue producing the same basic results at your current level of ability, or you could work to develop and improve. Of course, learning a skill is not just a matter of being told a set of techniques, but involves developing a better understanding of how processes work and why certain things are necessary.

The idea that you could develop a more in-depth and effective set of learning strategies is not actually all that surprising if you think about two things. Firstly, as mentioned in the previous section, scientists have been studying learning for many decades, so there is a good deal of detailed knowledge about how learning works. Granted, it's not perfect, but it's increasingly sophisticated and certainly a lot better than guess-work. Secondly (for most readers), you have not previously learned how to study, at least not in a way that is informed by detailed and up-to-date learning science. To return to the cooking analogy, it's like you have been shown how to use the microwave and just continue doing this repeatedly, when you could instead be learning how to make gourmet meals.

With any skill, people tend to acquire a set of comfortable strategies and stick with them. These strategies eventually become habits not because they work especially well but because they are familiar and easy, and have never seriously been tested or put under scrutiny. It is hard to change such habits. A research study led by Veronica Yan of the University of California showed that simply trying out better learning strategies is not enough to get learners to adopt such strategies, even when they have resulted in major improvements in their learning. What does work is having an explanation of why some strategies are more effective than others (as you will find in this book), combined with experience of trying the strategies out for yourself. [1]

Therefore once you have established effective methods for taking good quality notes in and out of class, it's important to learn how to recognise what works and what doesn't in a way that is both practical and evidence-based. Having developed an understanding of how to learn, you will then be in a position to apply this to everyday study as well as to exam revision.

The ideas within this book apply to all subjects. Some aspects may be particularly important for subjects that involve a lot of note taking and reading, and remembering of factual information. However, anything that you have to learn and remember involves essentially the same mental apparatus. Your brain doesn't care if you are learning Physics or Art History—it still takes in knowledge and skills the same way.

Your learning situation

Naturally, every learner will find themselves in a different situation, with different demands and types of classes. I will try to keep all of the advice very practical, yet general enough that it can be applied to many different subjects and study contexts.

For simplicity, I will make certain assumptions:

- that you are a student (or pupil) of one or more subjects (I will mainly use the terms 'student' when talking about classes, and 'learner' in more general contexts).
- that you have a teacher, lecturer, or tutor (for simplicity I will tend to use the term 'teacher' to cover all of these options). For students who are home-educated and learning with family support, a parent might play this role.
- that there are classes or lectures of some kind, during which you have a reasonable degree of freedom over how to take notes in a limited amount of time. I will refer to all such sessions as 'classes' (if you don't actually have formal classes—for example, for students working through self-directed online learning such as a MOOC course—the vast majority of strategies in the book will still apply).
- that you generally take notes either during classes or when studying alone, or both. For consistency I will refer to 'notebooks', though of course this also covers jotters, blank paper, and so forth.
- that you have access to a textbook or set of course-approved information of some kind, and perhaps online access to slides or other materials.
- that you are working towards at least one test or exam. This book is about initial learning as well as exam revision, and both will be discussed throughout.

If any of these assumptions don't apply to you, I think you will find that most of the advice still holds regardless, though you may need to make some adjustments and skip parts that don't fit with your situation—for example, if all of your classes are discussion-based and you are not encouraged to take notes, or if there is no relevant textbook at all in your subject.

Using this book

The next chapter outlines some of the biggest errors people make when they study. The rationale for including these at the start of the book is that most people will have at least some current learning and studying practices that they should reconsider. Research suggests that flawed strategies are extremely common among students, even though they are linked to getting poorer grades.[2]

Chapter 3 sets this into the context of learning science by presenting an overview of the principles that explain how people learn. This chapter is necessarily quite technical in places and can be skipped if you're in a hurry, though you will want to refer back to it—particularly when it comes to investigating your own learning habits (if time is really short, skip straight onto Chapter 9, which covers strategies for the last few days before your exam!).

Chapter 4 sets out clear strategies for note taking and making the most of your reading. After all, there's not much point in developing good learning strategies without first making sure that what you are learning is thorough and accurate! The subsequent chapters (Chapters 5 to 7) run through all practical aspects of learning, from retaining facts more effectively, to scheduling your study habits, to staying focused. Chapters 8 to

9 present an evidence-informed take on the preparation you should do prior to your exam. Finally, Chapter 10 encourages you to take the time to investigate these processes yourself, gathering evidence in your own context via self-tests and experiments, and guides you through this process.

To help you understand the new ideas and insights, each chapter begins with a set of questions that you should think about before reading. There are review questions at the end of each chapter, with answers at the end of the book.

I have, of course, aimed to make this book as up to date and accurate as possible and all key claims about research are supported with references to academic research, but as this is not a textbook I have tried to take a 'light touch' approach to such sources to improve readability. Please contact me via my website if you feel that research has been misrepresented or omitted, and I will be happy to review this for future editions.

2

Flawed strategies, and why they are failing you

What are the most popular learning and revision strategies?
Are re-reading and highlighting useful ways of learning?
What is 'overlearning'?

Before moving on to the effective learning strategies that are the primary focus of this book, let's think about some of the strategies that don't work so well. Often, these are not completely useless—it's just that they are associated with a lot of time and effort for relatively little payoff. In some cases, they also lead to rapid forgetting, so that the hard-earned learning disappears before you get a chance to use it in the real world.

Mindless copying

Sometimes, especially when you're tired, you may find yourself copying from a book into your notes, but realise that very little information is going in during the process. If you aren't focused on the meaning of the text and doing something with which you are actively engaged, you will remember very little at the end of the day. Granted, you will have a more complete set of notes—but that information was in the textbook anyway.

Worse still is the illusion of studying gained by photocopying books or downloading/bookmarking articles. It feels like you're learning, but unless you have a concrete plan for when to actively study this material, it can amount to little more than procrastination. In practice, there isn't going to be a day/week/month in the future where you have nothing else to do than read through all those files that you saved in the past! It would be better to write at least a short summary of each one at the time—doing so means that you have fully engaged with the material, and doesn't prevent you from making more detailed notes later.

Likewise, simply sitting in a class or lecture doesn't guarantee learning, and neither does copying slides down into your notebook (or highlighting notes—see below). Of course, most students enjoy copying from slides during a class, or take photos of them, because it feels like they are making progress. Direct copying may help to keep you awake, but you will be gaining relatively little in terms of learning from doing it—if anything. It's better to engage with the class in other ways, for example by asking questions, and then write summaries of the concepts covered in class later, in your own words. When it comes to notes, there are better ways of getting a good-quality set of information to revise from (this is discussed in Chapter 4).

Overall, it's really important to process new information actively and deeply. There is no way around this—you simply can't learn effectively if you're on autopilot. So if you find your eyes scanning the pages while you are thinking of something else, or take classroom notes in the hope that somehow or other the information will go in without any effort, then reconsider. It will be much more valuable to skip the copying and actively engage with the material.

Cramming

Cramming is the term often used for last-minute, intensive memorisation before an exam or test. Usually this focuses on texts such as a student's class notes, though it could also involve rapid memorisation of facts written on flashcards. Who hasn't seen at least one student outside an exam flicking through a set of index cards, or frantically trying to speed-read a textbook?

As a form of study, cramming leads to things becoming more accessible without actually being learned any better. This is because of two key things—it focuses on repetition, and it is compressed in time (which is termed *massed study*) rather than spaced out. Typically, cramming will also focus on rather shallow processing strategies, such as saying phrases over and over to yourself (which places the emphasis on the sound and wording of items, rather than on their meaning).

Real learning, in contrast, involves things being stored better in memory, not simply making them temporarily easier to access. This might seem a contradiction—but it is easy to understand if you consider how quickly something fades from memory if you don't ensure it is permanently stored. Think about how you can remember the names of characters in a mediocre movie well enough to follow and understand what's going on, but will then forget them pretty rapidly. In a similar way, cramming makes things temporarily more accessible, but doesn't ensure long-term storage. Things can also be effectively stored but hard to access—for example, the names of children and teachers from your primary/elementary school years are certainly stored in your long-term memory but might be hard to recall in the here and now. As a student, you ideally want things to be both securely stored in memory and accessible.

Psychology researcher Nate Kornell found that even when students were given a chance to try out a more effective technique, they preferred their traditional methods based around short-term cramming. That's right—even when they had tried something that worked better, learners didn't believe that it helped.[3] This is because we are very strongly influenced by past beliefs and habits, and it's hard to change people's beliefs even if you show them the evidence (think of how hard it is to change someone's political beliefs, for example!).

However, an important aspect of cramming is that it does work quite well over the short-term. If you only have a couple of days to prepare, cramming might be your best choice—and indeed, the only realistic option. But over the course of a year, for example, it's a hugely inefficient way to learn. It takes a lot of time, and leads to a lot of forgetting. To put it another way, cramming makes information more accessible but this is temporary, and the brief boost in performance does not lead to secure learning over the long term. The simple fact is that by selecting more effective strategies and study schedules you could spend much less time studying, and still come to know a lot more. In fact, if you study effectively, you shouldn't need to do much last-minute revision at all.

Overlearning

Another fixture of most classrooms, textbooks and revision sessions is what psychologists call *overlearning*. This is where you keep studying something beyond the point that you have already understood and mastered it. One of the clearest examples of this can be seen on the pages of most traditional mathematics textbooks—usually, these show multiple examples of the same type of problem, sometimes twenty or more. Clearly if someone can answer the first ten, they have already 'got' the concept, and further practice is therefore considered to be overlearning.

Again, overlearning relates to a flawed metaphor of how memory works. Educators in the past treated children's learning a bit like the training of a dog—they felt it was necessary to keep practicing habits so that they didn't get forgotten. However, children are different to dogs in many ways (as you may have noticed!). Once you've got the point of something, doing further practice straight away is essentially a waste of time

The futility of overlearning was well illustrated in an experiment by Doug Rohrer and Kelly Taylor of the University of South Florida. They taught students about a maths concept, and then gave them a set of practice tasks to try. One group was given nine tasks, and the other was given just three. After the first three tasks, the average success rate for both groups was around 90%—meaning that tasks 4–9 (for those who did them) involved overlearning. What's interesting is that when tested four weeks later on a new set of tasks, there were no differences between how the groups performed. The 'nine tasks' group had worked for three times as long, and gained absolutely nothing for their efforts.

Re-reading

Another flawed study strategy is re-reading—that is, reading over a set of notes or textbook pages repeatedly. This can result in an increased sense of fluency and confidence with the material in the book. However, it doesn't necessarily mean that it has been any better learned.

Again, students tend to assume that reading something again is an effective way to secure it in memory. This is a good example of how our *metacognitive beliefs* about our own learning and knowledge can be flawed. Many people think they know what is working for them in terms of study, but these judgements tend to be based on a perception of how easy it feels, and how quickly they are making progress.[4] Unfortunately, these rules of thumb are not very good ways of judging learning! In fact, if study feels very easy, this usually indicates that not much is being learned, because the material has already been mastered.

Again, this has been studied systematically. Researchers have compared the performance of students who read over a chapter once with those who read the same chapter twice, and found no difference.[5] And re-reading can be viewed as another form of overlearning—which, as we have just seen, is largely a waste of time.

It's important to distinguish this sort of re-reading from cases where the material was not well understood the first time around. If that is the case, then it will be valuable to read the information again and try to develop a clearer understanding.

But once information has been fully understood, reading it over again won't help very much—it would be better to test yourself on it instead (see Chapter 5).

Highlighting

Highlighter pens are fun—they make your notes look more interesting. Coloured text has to be more memorable, right?

Wrong. The sad truth is that highlighting a text makes very little difference to how much you remember (if it did, textbook publishers would simply print all of their books on yellow backgrounds!) As we will see in the next chapter, research on deep processing in long-term memory has shown that shallow, surface-level processing, such as the appearance of words, has little lasting effect. It's much more valuable to focus on the meaning of information than what it looks like.

The idea that the appearance of text makes little difference to memory was understood by researcher Allan Paivio as early as the 1960s. He was curious about an earlier finding that people remember a picture (e.g. a picture of an apple) better than the equivalent word (e.g. the word 'apple'). One prevailing explanation was that the picture was more vivid, and therefore made a more lasting impression. In an attempt to test this theory, Paivio and his colleagues showed people words or black & white pictures either with or without colours added. They found that added colour made no difference to recall [6] (for the rest of the story about why pictures are remembered better than words, see Chapter 5!).

There is a glimmer of hope for the manufacturers of high-lighter pens, however. Highlighting can be effective—if we use it right. Colouring in large blocks of text is likely to have little benefits because it is insufficiently active as a task. But according to a 2014 study by Carole Yue and colleagues, it can be beneficial if the highlighting involves picking out specific phrases or words, and colour coding them.[7] This may prompt learners to think deeply about the key ideas, categorising and comparing information. Importantly, the study found that highlighting did not impair memory for the non-highlighted text. It is likely that underlining would have similar benefits if used strategically.

Review questions

1. What is the key problem associated with cramming, and when can it be useful?
2. What similarity is there between overlearning and re-reading?
3. What can be done to make highlighting more effective?

3

What is learning?

What is the role of short-term memory when we study?
Are different types of information stored in different ways?
What is the role of different types of study task in terms of how well we remember things?

L et's start with a brief of overview of how successful learning works. This will focus on how you think and the actions that you take, rather than on the brain; although there is no doubt that the brain is the organ that makes thinking and memory possible, you don't need to know about neuroscience to be an effective student.

An overview of how learning works

As a learner, you need to experience information, ideas and skills in some way, such as through reading or via a lecture. After this, there are two key things that can happen. The most common scenario is that much of the information is forgotten. Alternatively, you—or a teacher—could take action to ensure that new information is consolidated in some way. That is, it will be used or revised such that it forms a new long-term memory (and more importantly, such that it links to your existing knowledge).

Even having information in memory is not enough—you need to be able to use it. This ability to *transfer* learning to new situations is often vital in exams, for example where you are shown scenarios or examples and have to identify them. Increasingly, educators are moving towards types of exam where learners have to show that they understand and can use ideas, rather than recalling them word for word (see Chapter 9). These can involve scenarios which you haven't seen prior to the exam, requiring you to think on your feet. Successful learning is therefore *not* about memorising lists of content or prepared answers. It is about developing a sound, flexible understanding of new ideas that you can use in multiple ways. In time, such transfer becomes almost effortless.

Misconceptions about memory

It's worth mentioning at this point that unless you have previously studied cognitive psychology, it's likely that you have a slightly flawed idea of how memory works.

Try the following task. Which of these things are true? Test yourself, and then look at the explanation below:

1. Human memory works like a computer hard-drive
2. Nothing enters memory unless you pay attention to it
3. Revision for an exam mainly involves short-term memory
4. Forgetting is the main problem facing learners

5. Memorisation primarily depends on repetition of informa-
    tion
6. Learning involves creating a file in long-term memory
    which is new and separate from existing knowledge
7. Forgetting mainly occurs due to the passing of time.

All right, how did you get on? It may strike you that these are
quite difficult things to say for sure—a response which in itself
shows the need for research into memory, and for basing study
habits on science.

If you were paying attention, you'll have noticed that one of
these issues (item five) was raised in the introductory chapter
to this book—memorising things is not just down to repetition, and indeed repetition alone is an ineffective strategy for
ensuring that new ideas are well remembered. Clearly more
practice is better than less, and where information is repeated,
you will have more of a chance to take it in compared to seeing
it only once. But much more important is what you do with the
information each time you study it. Exactly what you should
be doing to better take in the information is discussed and
explained throughout this book, particularly during Chapter
5.

In terms of the other items, the answers are:

1. False—human memory does not work like a computer
    hard-drive. There are many important ways that your
    memory differs from a computer—not least the fact that
    you usually need to work at learning in order to remember
    something, rather than just hitting 'save'!
2. True—attention is essential to memory. There are some

minor exceptions, but for nearly everything you study, you do need to focus attention in order to be successful (sadly, you can't learn from playing a podcast during your sleep).

3. False. Short-term memory only holds information for a matter of seconds or minutes, so everything that you write down in an exam hall is coming from long-term memory. A good example of using short-term memory is reading the number from your bank card, and then typing it into a shopping website. This example also shows how limited this store is in terms of size—you can't hold all 16 digits of a credit card number in short-term memory, and therefore have to check back to your card midway through.

4. True—and false. Forgetting is inevitable, and clearly we want to remember what we study, not forget it. However, forgetting is not as much of an enemy of learning as you might think. In fact, at times I will encourage you to deliberately delay restudy in ways that will increase forgetting, because this is more beneficial over the long-term. Again, more on this in later chapters.

5. As noted above, this is false.

6. False. Remember, memory is not like a computer hard drive. Memories link together—a memory that is separate from everything else in your mind is essentially pretty useless. So your long-term memories are not separate items (contrary to the way they are presented in the movie *Inside Out*). It's not helpful to try memorising isolated facts, because learning involves connecting and understanding ideas. And a lot of learning involves reorganising what you know, rather than forming entirely new memories.

7. While time is an issue, forgetting is not only or even mainly due to time passing. Forgetting can be managed, and loss

of knowledge is more due to failing to understand and use information, rather than being the inevitable consequence of time.

Another very common misconception about learning is that we all have a particular 'learning style', and that identifying and studying according to this style will lead to better results. The most common claim is that there are three type of learners: kinaesthetic (movement-based), visual and auditory, though there are other versions of the theory. However, there is general agreement in psychology that this idea is a myth. If you think you will learn better via visual information, it may be that you do—but not because you're a visual learner. Learning via videos and diagrams will be helpful for everyone, because it combines visual and verbal information (see Chapter 5). In fact, everyone's memory works in an essentially similar way. While we do have real differences in our abilities and existing knowledge, our minds are all fundamentally alike, meaning that the science-based approaches to learning apply to everyone.

The most appropriate type of learning task also depends more on the information than the learner. For example, it makes sense to learn maps visually, to learn novels via reading and discussing them, and to learn sports by doing them. Imagine trying to learn to drive purely by hearing an explanation of the process—it really doesn't make sense! However, as all of these examples also demonstrate, a combination of learning tasks will often be more useful than trying to find a single best learning style—for example, trying out a sport, but also looking at diagrams and hearing verbal instructions (simultaneously kinaesthetic, visual and auditory).

Short-term 'working' memory

As noted above, students often incorrectly assume that studying is all about putting information into the short-term memory (STM). This is untrue—in fact, what psychologists refer to as STM is actually a tiny store, which can only hold a few pieces of information for a very short time. If you revise the night before an exam, you are not putting the information into short-term memory. You are probably not putting it into memory at all.

However, STM is vitally important as a gateway into long-term memory (LTM), as information needs to be processed in the here-and-now before it can be permanently stored. It's therefore much more important for learning and studying than it is for exam recall.

STM nowadays tends to be called *working memory*, because its functions are all about taking in and processing information, and doing real tasks. For example, if you listen to a drinks order from a few friends and then go to the bar to order the drinks, then you are using your working memory. It is very limited in size, and the information is easily forgotten—as we have all experienced, when needing to ask someone to repeat something that they said only a few moments ago.

Working memory is also more than just a mental store for information. It has several components, each of which can deal with different types of information. Most importantly to students, we have verbal working memory and visual working memory, allowing us to separately process or combine verbal and visual information. It is relatively easy to do a visual task such as driving at the same time as a verbal task such as holding a conversation. However, it is extremely difficult to do two tasks that use the same part of working memory—for example, holding a conversation while reading an email. These limitations affect the best way to study, as will be discussed later.

Long-term memory

Long-term memory (LTM) is often seen as the brain's filing cabinet, where information is stored until you need it. However, this gives a misleading impression: it wrongly suggests that such information remains stored in the same form, unchanged and not affecting new learning. In fact, information in LTM is easily distorted. As psychologist Robert Bjork has said, every time we recall a piece of information, we change it in some way.[8]

From a study perspective, the forgetting and distortion of information both happen rapidly in LTM. Even within a few minutes, people generally fail to recall the exact words that they heard, and only remember the general meaning. If the information was meaningless, then they will recall next to nothing.

Prior learning also affects new learning. This can be observed in terms of how easily an expert takes in new information compared to a beginner. This shows you that the process of learning is not a one-way street, that is, it's not a matter of just absorbing information from the outside world and storing it in some kind of memory file. Instead, your current knowledge is used to make sense of new things that you experience and read about.

One of the key processes that happens when we make sense of new learning is a process of categorisation. Developmental psychologist Jean Piaget believed that babies and young children form new categories as they explore the world, gradually realising (through play and experience) which things are similar to one another and which are separate.[9] As they do so, they form mental models of each new concept, which gradually increase in complexity. Psychologists call this kind of mental model a *schema*.

As you learn, new information can be added to this model to make a more fully developed schema. This essentially means that all usable information in long-term memory is interlinked. New learning is defined in terms of how it fits with your existing knowledge—or how it differs.

It's worth noting that a schema is much more than just a dictionary definition. For example, the Cambridge Dictionary defines a restaurant as "a place where meals are prepared and served to customers".[10] Your schema knowledge about a restaurant is much more sophisticated than this. For example, you know that you need to take some money with you when you go to a restaurant, and that you often need to contact them in advance to get a table, and that you generally wait to be seated in some sorts of restaurant but not others, and dozens of other things. In other words, your knowledge of the concept is complex, and is linked to your understanding of how life works in the society and culture where you live.

There are two further really important things to know about LTM. One is that its capacity is basically limitless. There is no point at which your memory gets full (if it feels this way, this is probably just tiredness!).

What's more—and this may be surprising—information that has been well learned doesn't get forgotten. It is all still in there somewhere, provided that you fully took it in and understood it. However—and this will be less of a surprise—this information becomes harder to access if it is not used.

In light of the last two points, one way of thinking about a piece of information in your long-term memory is that it is like an object buried in a large pit of sand, and gradually sinking. With time, it will sink so deeply that it will be very difficult to find. However, if you have used the information recently, it will only be buried at a very shallow level, and so will be easy to uncover with a bit of digging around.

From a revision point of view, this means that there is little point in revising something you have gone over recently. It will be much more valuable to go over something that is 'deep in the sand'—i.e. something that you have almost forgotten. Doing so will make much more of a difference, bringing a hard-to-access item much closer to the surface.

Making more meaningful links to an item also makes it easier to retrieve—almost as if you have map to the item's location. In contrast, an item which is isolated and not connected to any of your prior knowledge is very easily 'lost' (i.e. forgotten).

Depth of processing

As mentioned earlier, there are many ways in which the mind differs from a computer. One such difference lies in the way in which we think about (or 'process') information. In a computer, processing is largely a separate issue to storage. However in your memory, the way you think about information makes a big difference to how well you will remember it in future. In particular, processing which focuses on the meaning of information leads to it being better remembered than processing based on more superficial characteristics, such as a word's appearance or sound. This is known as *depth of processing*. This may be in part because the meaningful links to other memories make it easier to access (see previous section).

A fascinating demonstration of this come from a series of research studies in the 1970s, led by Scottish psychologist Fergus Craik. In one study, student participants were asked to look at a list of words and answer a question about each word. Some questions prompted the students to think about the meaning, for example, 'Is it a type of flower? Daisy'. Other questions prompted the students to think about the sound of the word (e.g. 'Does it rhyme with *rote*? Boat' or about the appearance of the word ('Is it in upper case letters?'). Answers could be either true or false—what mattered was whether the students were prompted to think about the meaning, or something else about the word. Findings showed that regardless of the individual words used, recall was better if participants had been asked about something to do with the meaning than either of the other two variations. Asking about the appearance of words led to the worst level of recall on a later test (fitting with the points made about highlighting in Chapter 2).

A similar study asked participants to process meaning by asking if words would fit a particular sentence frame. For example, which of the following would fit here?

Possible words: rabbit; helpful
Sentence frame: The eagle caught the _____.

Clearly the word 'rabbit' makes sense, and the word 'helpful' does not. But the question can only be answered if you think about what the words mean. It's even more effective for memory if the sentence frame is elaborate ('The eagle swooped down and snatched the struggling _____'), and if it's visual rather than abstract (the previous example is much more visual than a frame such as 'A _____ is a life form'). Best of all, the processing should combine elements of self-reference i.e. drawing on your own opinions and experiences, and prompt you to generate your own response rather than simply respond to information (e.g. completing the sentence, 'A _____ is the type of animal that I'd most like to have as a pet').

One reason that generating a word is helpful to memory is that it's also helpful to think *actively* about new concepts if we want to remember them. Unfortunately, many traditional learning situations are rather passive. They don't involve actually doing very much—just listening to a teacher/lecturer or reading information. Of course, you may be very mentally active while you attend a lecture or read a book (this will vary a lot from person to person). But the situation doesn't force you to engage. In some cases, you may be listening with just a fraction of your attention and working memory capacity, while the rest focuses on something else—such as what an attractive fellow student nearby is doing.

In contrast, solving a problem or puzzle is an inherently active task. There is no way to engage with these sorts of learning experiences without thinking actively and in a way that largely occupies your working memory. For this reason, lectures that include frequent short tasks or questions throughout the session lead to students focusing better.[11]

Of course, you can't force your teacher or textbook writer to include questions, but you can take notes in a way that prompts you to keep thinking actively—for example, by summarising the content rather than copying down entire phrases from slides or textbook pages. Well-designed gap-fill tasks have the benefit of combining active processing with the benefits of deep processing discussed earlier in this section.

Two types of long-term memory

As we have seen, it's important to understand and focus on the meaning of information. However, it's also important to remember details. Researcher Endel Tulving (a colleague of Fergus Craik—they worked together on the depth of processing research) established that there are two main types of factual memories—memory for specific events, and memory for general concepts. These are called *episodic memories* and *semantic memories*, respectively. For example, a memory of visiting the Alps on holiday is an episodic memory, but retaining knowledge of that mountain range in general—such as where it is, how it was formed, how high the mountains are compared to other mountain ranges—is a semantic memory.

Traditional theories of learning assumed that we learn details as specific 'episodes' (for example, a time that we saw a mountain on a nature program) and over time use these to form a general schema (we have learned the features of a mountain in general, regardless of specific examples). That is to say, you experience multiple specific events (which could include reading an example in a book or being told a specific detail by a teacher), and over time you combine these into more general knowledge in the form of one or more schemas. According to this view, episodic memories provide detailed, specific information but also allow us to gradually develop meaningful semantic memories.

That may all sound rather complex, but the key idea is that our meaningful mental models or schemas are based on semantic memory, and that they develop gradually via multiple learning experiences. Having a general understanding (rather than a few context-specific memories) helps us to transfer general ideas to new situations, too.

Coming to understand the meaning of a new concept is highly important, but clearly, as a student, it is also necessary to remember some specific details. When studying anatomy, for example, a doctor needs to know how arteries, bones and infection work in general, but they must also remember the names of specific bones, or the symptoms of a particular disease.

Getting a little bit deeper in to the research before we move on, a more recent theory of memory and thinking called *fuzzy trace theory* (devised by Charles Brainerd and Valerie Reyna) proposes that rather than semantic memories being a kind of averaged version of multiple episodic memories, the two things are actually learned simultaneously—it's just that the details of an episodic memory are forgotten much more rapidly.[12] So you may find that although you tend to remember the gist of a class pretty well a week later, you have typically forgotten some of the key terminology after just a few hours. To use the sandpit analogy (see LTM section, above), some memories sink faster than others (in part this may be because specific words and terminology are often rather arbitrary, and hard to link to other meaningful memories). In practice, this means that details and terminology should be revised and consolidated sooner than other types of learning.

Review questions

1. Name one popular misconception about memory.
2. What happens when we try to use two different parts of working memory at the same time?
3. What are the two key types of long-term memory?
4. Which type of memory should be revised soonest—gist or

detail?

4

Study habits

What should you do during a class?
What's the most efficient way to tackle course reading and establish a set of study notes?
What are flashcards for, and how should you use them?

Before we move on to how you should hack your memory and boost learning, let's look at getting the right information in the most effective way. After all, if you are going to study for a test or exam, you need a good, complete set of materials with all the right information. You will want to build a set of well-organised notes, but as discussed above, simply copying from slides is not very helpful when it comes to remembering the information taught in class, and it's not the most reliable way of making notes, either.

So, what should you do in class, as well as during your revision, in order to develop accurate, complete notes, and to learn well while doing do? Let's look at how to do this best, focusing on understanding and staying motivated during the process.

During classes and lectures

Is your current classroom note-taking approach working? To answer this question we have to think what exactly do we mean by 'working'. I would define this as a strategy which takes good quality notes in the minimum possible time, and frees up as much attention as possible for other tasks such as engaging with class activities.

Consider the following two scenarios:

Amina takes careful notes during every class, copying down items from PowerPoint slides, as well as summarising what the class tutor says. When it comes to exam time, she largely revises from her textbook.

Ben doesn't take many notes, and his notebook is usually quite messy. It largely contains responses to tasks set during class. When he studies, he tries to make sense of these, filling in the many gaps by looking things up in his textbook.

Both of the students described above have significant flaws with their classroom note-taking strategies. Amina works hard to establish a good set of notes during class, but then doesn't really use them to study at a later date. If she would rather study from her book, it would make more sense for her to skip the note-taking during class, or at least to take minimal key points and quotes that could later be combined with the textbook information.

Ben, on the other hand, doesn't really take notes at all. It's fine to have a class notebook which is largely focused on responses to class activities. However, Ben's mistake is to attempt to use this as a revision tool. It would make more sense to ignore his class notes entirely, and to make a fresh set of neat study notes from his textbook, or from a set of class slides.

Regardless of the note-taking approach used, it's possible that mistakes can creep in. It would be a good idea to fact-check any notes for errors and omissions, because otherwise you may revise things which are actually incorrect! In my experience, very few students ask their tutor to look over their study notes. I have been happy to do this when asked—and even if a teacher declines to do so, there's nothing lost by asking. An alternative would be to team up with 2–3 fellow students to check each other's notes. A diligent friend may well notice if you have missed or misunderstood a key area of content.

Alternative note-taking formats

The obvious way of taking notes is in a linear fashion, noting one point after another down the page, in the same way as you would write a short description or essay. However, another format that is becoming more popular is the *Cornell notes system* (named after Cornell University, an Ivy League university in New York, where it was devised). The system involves dividing each side of a page into three sections, usually by drawing a horizontal line two thirds of the way down the page to create a separate section at the bottom of the page, and then dividing the top section into two halves with a vertical line. One of the upper sections is used for normal notes during class. The other side is for noting down keywords and key questions at the end. This can be done as a whole class if the teacher and fellow students are on board with the Cornell system, or by yourself. Finally, the section at the bottom of the page is for a summary of the whole lesson.

Again this can be done later—perhaps summarising the whole week's classes during a 1-hour study session at the weekend, for example.

One great thing about the Cornell system is its simplicity—any sheet of paper will do. It also has the advantage of organisation—it helps to identify and emphasise key words and questions, and the summary provides a higher-level overview which is completed with the benefit of time to reflect, and which can be used as a prompt for later study.

Another popular form of note taking is to use mind maps or concept maps. These can have the benefit of combining visual and verbal information (see Chapter 5), although they are rather time consuming to do. As such they are again best completed after class rather than during it. But be realistic—are you really going to write a mind map on the basis of every single class? Is that a habit that you will stick to beyond the first couple of weeks? And does it fit with the principles described in the previous section in terms of getting the best outcome with the least effort? These questions are worth considering in light of your own habits and preferences. My recommendation is to use concept maps for higher-level summaries (see later section of this chapter) rather than for every class.

Taking notes from books

Taking notes from books or school-provided materials (such as hand-outs) has many advantages over doing so during a class—you have more time to think the material through, are less likely to make mistakes, and can take time to check or look up anything that's unclear.

However, again you need to be realistic—don't leave this all to the last minute, or it simply won't get done! Purely in terms of workload, it's essential to develop a strategy that gets the work done via a little-and-often approach rather than leaving it until the week or two before your exam. Fortunately, that sort of approach also helps you to establish new semantic memories more effectively, too (see Chapter 3).

Learning is most effective when it is active, and there is a danger that reading can become a passive activity with a lack of attention and focus. Two key approaches can help to tackle this. One is to aim to learn particular things, rather than just get through the reading. So at the outset, write a set of questions that you hope to answer from reading a particular chapter or section (this book provides some for you at the start of each chapter—an example of this technique at work!).

An old but effective approach is *skimming* quickly through the text once, to gain an overview (rather than to find a particular word or section), before going back to read it all again in more detail.[13] Skimming is a skill that anyone can develop, and is in fact the basis of speed reading—exceptionally fast readers skim the text, and combine this with their prior understanding of the topic. As might be expected, your level of understanding of a text will drop when you skim rather than read for detail, but there is still enough understanding, when combined with prior knowledge, to get a gist overview in around a third of the time it would take to read normally. This way, you develop the beginnings of an understanding of the key issues or concepts, and it's therefore easier to make sense of these when you read them again in detail. This re-reading should also be faster due to better understanding, meaning that the whole process needn't take any longer.

The issue of how best to take notes from books is a deep

one—there is a lot of research on this topic alone—but again, it's important to be pragmatic. Investigate how long your current ideal strategy would take if you spent that much time on every book section. Do you have that much time to spare? If so, is this the best way to spend it? These are important decisions to make for you as a learner.

If in doubt, aim to take notes from your textbook that capture the key concepts at quite a high level, even if this means you miss out some of the details. And above all, remember that regularly taking a functional set of notes from your book, even if they are not perfect, is a lot better than not doing the reading at all—or trying to read it all the day before an exam!.

Transforming your notes

Writing a set of notes based on your classes or textbook is an important stage, but it is really only the beginning. Hopefully you have now begun to form a strategy that will help you to develop an effective, easy-to-use set of notes, taken steps to ensure its accuracy, and been pragmatic about the time required to consolidate these notes and combine them with textbook reading.

At the end of the day, though, you need to do more than just make an excellent set of notes—you need to find ways of getting the key information into your memory in a form that can be used for practical situations. The notes themselves can't answer your exam questions for you (and even for open-book assessments, it's highly beneficial to have key information memorised).

I strongly recommend making use of flashcards for detailed information and review questions, and concept maps/mindmaps to show overall topic summaries.

Making up flashcards should involve writing a key term, sentence or quote onto an index card or similar small piece of card/paper. Online flashcards could also be used. The key points could be selected from the main questions and summaries from each page of Cornell-style notes, or from points identified when reading (see above).

Having written a suitable item on one side of the flashcard, what goes on the other? In my view, this should show a question or similar prompt that makes it possible to test yourself, so that you are not simply reading the key points. Such self-testing should be challenging but not impossible. In this way, you can look through a set of questions one at a time, test your ability to answer them, and then flip over each flashcard to check your responses were accurate (either immediately, or after looking at all of the questions).

Having a key item plus question on each flashcard makes it easy to reorder the cards, and drop (for later study sessions) items that have already been well learned so that you are not wasting time on overlearning. More information can be added where necessary, and questions and prompts can be modified if they are too easy or too difficult (remember—challenging but not impossible!). Because of the ease and flexibility of this system, I recommend having only one item—in particular one question/prompt—per card, although the response information could have sub-items. Some examples are as follows:

What's the capital of Malta? Valletta
What are the bones of the human wrist? Scaphoid, lunate, triquetrum, pisiform, trapezium, trapezoid, capitate, hamate.
Trigonometry letters? SOH CAH TOA
Name of Stanford Prison experiment researcher? Philip

Zimbardo.

Quote by Hamlet on the human condition? *"What a piece of work is man, How noble in reason, how infinite in faculty, In form and moving how express and admirable, In action how like an Angel, In apprehension how like a god, The beauty of the world, The paragon of animals. And yet to me, what is this quintessence of dust? Man delights not me; no, nor Woman neither; though by your smiling you seem to say so."*

A flaw in using flashcards is that they encourage memorisation of isolated contact without emphasising the bigger picture of meaningful interconnection. This can be addressed by combining their use with the study of *concept maps*. A concept map is a type of mind map where key concepts are connected via lines, with each line representing a meaningful link. For a more sophisticated version, these lines could be drawn as arrows and labelled to indicate the relationship between two concepts, such being *x* being a part of *y*.

Concept maps typically differ from standard mind maps in that they do not include pictures, and there is no central concept to which all other items must connect. This makes them quicker to complete and more flexible. However, pictures can be added if you prefer, and may well be beneficial (see Chapter 5).

A concept map can be an excellent way of getting an overview of a whole topic. However, depending on how advanced your course is, you may prefer to focus on a subtopic. An introductory Chemistry student may do a concept map on hydrocarbons, for example, but a more advanced student might do one on a specific type of hydrocarbon, such as on alkenes. If you won't fit an entire topic into a concept map, it's important to maintain the overall structure, and this can be done by including notes that show how the subtopic links to other areas of study that are not included.

Studying with flashcards can therefore be combined with drawing up and studying concept maps—one helps you to learn the detailed information from your course, and the other shows the overall picture, and how these details link to one another. As with other areas of study, concept mapping is best when done actively rather than passively—creating a concept map from memory is of more value than copying one from a slide [14] (or worse still, printing one out).

Review questions

1. How can we judge whether our note-taking habits are working?
2. What are the three sections that feature on a page when using the Cornell notes system?
3. What does skimming a textbook chapter involve, and why might it be beneficial?
4. What's the best format for a study flashcard?

5

Making the learning last

What is the role of retrieval in studying, and when should I use it?

What is dual coding, and how can I incorporate it into my notes and learning?

How can I make the best use of elaborated examples?

H aving established good study notes and flashcards, you need a set of go-to strategies for helping the information to stick meaningfully in your memory, in a way that will last. This chapter will present three such strategies—retrieval practice, dual coding and elaborated examples.

Retrieval practice

As discussed in Chapter 3, it is a misconception that encoding information to memory is primarily a matter of repetition. In fact—as the research on overlearning shows—repetition is quite limited in its use. Certainly, you need to go over material more than once to be sure of learning it, and this is particularly true for difficult material and for details/terminology. But more important still is what you do during these repetitions.

Having initially come across a concept during class, an essential but much neglected principle is to actively retrieve the information from memory (rather than simply re-reading or highlighting it, as we have seen). All too often I see students reading textbooks, flicking through PowerPoints or screenshots, or highlighting class notes. They certainly look studious, but how much are they actually remembering?

Retrieval practice means the deliberate retrieval of information from memory, used as a study or learning strategy. This is not just a matter of self-testing to check your knowledge. It is the act of retrieval—bringing something back to mind—that secures the information in memory, helping to it become permanently learned. Retrieval can therefore be used to boost learning and to prevent forgetting.

It might seem counterintuitive that retrieval (rather than reading, for example) should lead to learning, given that nothing new is being presented, but there is good experimental evidence to support the idea. One superb study conducted by researchers Henry Roediger III and Jeffrey Karpicke in 2006 involved presenting learners with a text, and then asking them to do one of three things:

- Read the text again three times (re-reading group).
- Read the text two more times, then test themselves by writing down everything they could remember (mixed group).
- Not read the text again at all, but instead test themselves three times, by writing down everything they could remember on three occasions (testing group).

Which group did best? The answer is a little complex, but also very instructive. When tested on their recall and understanding after just five minutes, there was little difference between the groups, though the re-reading group were slightly better on average, and the testing group slightly worse. When tested after a week, though, these results were reversed! In other words, after enough time for forgetting to play a role, the testing group showed the best recall of ideas — even though they had only seen the original text once (compared to four times for the re-reading group).[15]

This is a powerful demonstration that re-reading is ineffective, and that for timescales that might be relevant in education (a test is more likely to be a week later than five minutes after learning), self-testing is an effective way to combat forgetting and make sure new learning sticks in the mind. It's also worth noting that none of the groups were given any feedback on the self-test. Had they been given feedback to allow them to improve their responses, it's likely that the self-test group would have done better still. Not only could they have corrected any mistakes, they would also have gained a better understanding of their own strengths and weaknesses, which could in turn guide their future learning.

Therefore, although we may think of tests as something teachers do to grade and judge their students, this is actually one of the least useful applications of tests (and least accurate, as it takes no account of what stage their learning is at). Instead, it is really valuable to regularly test your own comprehension by trying to bring information back to mind. Three ways of doing this, building on the ideas from the previous two chapters, are:

- Summarise the content of a class or lecture without referring to your notes

- Use flashcards (see previous chapter), to test your recall of finer details such as terminology
- Form concept maps from memory, rather than from notes

If you find these things difficult to do, then you have learned something useful—there are some things that you thought you knew, but actually didn't! Now you can go back and focus your attention on filling those gaps. And each time you successfully retrieve ideas or details, this is helping to build permanent memories.

Dual coding

As noted earlier, working memory is thought to have several different components, including a verbal and a visual store. These allow us to process words and images simultaneously, for example when watching a documentary. In long-term memory, too, theories have shifted from viewing memory as a single store to one that can store different types of memory. Following the work of psychologist Allan Paivio, it has become clear that images play a key role in LTM, too.

Chapter 3 discussed research dating back to the 1960s which showed that images or objects are better remembered than words. For example, if people are shown a set of everyday objects, they will later remember more of them than if they just read the same object names as a list—a finding that appears to apply to all age groups.[16] This is despite the fact that they are asked to recall the items verbally, and intuitively it might be assumed that converting mental images to words would make the task harder.

Paivio argued that the reason images are better recalled than words is because when we see a picture, we spontaneously think of the word as well. This is similar to the way you think of the sound of a word when you see a group of letters on the page. He argued that this led to dual coding—processing of both the image and word in memory.[17] Consequently, two separate memories are formed, leading to more chance of the information later being remembered—if one memory fails, the other might still act as a cue to recall. Interestingly, the reverse isn't true—seeing a word does not always lead to people spontaneously generating a mental image, but they can choose to do so as a learning strategy.

Paivio developed this idea into *dual coding theory* (DCT). Dual coding is the process of combining verbal materials with visual materials (which could include diagrams and interesting layouts, as well as actual pictures.) In education, there are many ways to visually represent material alongside words, including:

· illustrations
· concept maps (see previous chapter)
· graphs and charts
· sketches
· photographs
· images on powerpoint slides

However, DCT does more than just encourage the use of pictures in education. It suggests that both pictures and words, when encoded together, will create a stronger memory trace, including two distinct type of representation. Therefore, it will be easier to retrieve the item from memory, as either the word or image could provide sufficient information to trigger retrieval of an episodic memory.

Elaboration

Elaboration means making study material more distinctive and richly meaningful by adding extra detail and complexity. In Chapter 3, I described how a more active and elaborate sentence can lead to a word being better remembered than when the same word is seen in a simple sentence. Elaboration can also include ways of relating the item to your own life ('self-reference').

Students and teachers often overlook elaboration. Again, our instincts let us down—we want to make things as simple as possible. Numerous research studies have shown that we tend to remember things better if they are vivid and distinctive. You will perhaps recall that long-term memory thrives on meaning. Indeed, the key way that memory operates is by developing schemas—meaningfully interconnected mental models that can become more sophisticated via future learning.

A stereotype is a good example of an unsophisticated schema. If we have met very few people from Scotland, we might have an idea of Scots that comes largely from clichéd presentations in adverts or movies—someone with red hair and a kilt, perhaps, like the lead character Jamie Fraser in the TV show *Outlander*. However, as we meet and get to know real Scottish people, new learning makes our schema become much more sophisticated—indeed, we may learn to make distinctions among different groups of Scots, such as the differences between people who live in different areas of Glasgow. Such schemas are still stereotyped to an extent, but they are more accurate and based on real experiences. In a similar way, our learning throughout the school years gradually moves beyond childish notions and gets closer to scientific understandings.

One great way of elaborating on new concepts is to find and

44

discuss examples. In my social psychology classes on the topic of obedience, I encourage learners to observe and blog about examples of obedience in everyday life. They try to link the features that make obedience more or less likely to occur to the processes and research they have studied in class. A similar strategy could be used in most subjects, from Physics to Politics.

A closely related concept is the use of *concreteness*. This is where you find a way of describing things in a way that is real and can be visualised (e.g. the 1918 flu pandemic killed 50 million people in Europe) rather than more abstract (e.g. pandemics often kill a lot of people). This aspect of elaboration makes use of the dual coding advantage (visual & verbal material being better remembered than verbal alone), combining the benefits of visuals with more elaborate meaning.

An elaborated example can really help learning to stick. Ensure that all of the key concepts in your notes and/or flashcards feature at least one such example, which can be illustrated with an image to further boost your recall. There is one important caveat here—it's easy to get an example wrong! Amanda Zamary and colleagues at Kent State University looked at student-generated examples and found that they were often flawed, missing key aspects of the studied concept.[18] This doesn't mean that creating examples is a bad idea, but that these examples will only be as good as your current level of understanding. As you learn more, the examples will get more sophisticated—so keep revisiting and trying to improve them.

Review questions

1. After what timescale did participants in Roediger & Karpicke's experiment do better after repeated testing

(rather than repeated re-reading)?

2. Why might a visual image alone be better remembered than a word alone?

3. Give <u>one</u> thing that might make an example on one of your flashcards more elaborate.

6

The importance of your study schedule

Which is preferable—studying something soon after it was first learned, or waiting until information has been partially forgotten?

Why might it be useful to interleave/mix up different types of practice questions?

The previous chapter looked at what to do when you study, and this one looks at a much neglected but equally important issue—when to do it!

Like many aspects of learning, the process of planning and scheduling your study time is an area on which most students receive little or no guidance, and what advice they do receive may well be informed more by common-sense beliefs than by evidence. Here we will look at the science of timing as it applies to learning and revision.

In particular, this chapter focuses on two key effects: the *spacing effect*—the reliable finding that extending the gap between study and restudy makes the process more effective, and *interleaving*—the benefits of mixing up practice items, rather than studying several examples of the same concept in a block.

You may be reading this guide with your exam a fortnight away, and think that this section therefore doesn't apply. Wait! There is still much to be gained from spacing and interleaving, even over shorter timescales. Research studies with young children have shown that a spacing effect gap of even a couple of minutes has benefits in terms of remembering items better.[19] Spacing and interleaving can certainly be used within study sessions, as well as in-between them. However you will also want to focus particularly on Chapter 11, which describes how to apply the techniques in the immediate run up to an exam.

Spacing

A key weapon in the battle to learn more effectively is the spacing effect. This has nothing to do with physical space—it is where information is spaced out over time, with practice occurring minutes, days or even weeks after an initial study session. It's very important to understand that the effect applies to all types of learning, regardless of the subject or topic (and has even been demonstrated in animals).

It no doubt seems a little counterintuitive to suggest that you should wait longer until restudying something. It seems to run against common beliefs, such as 'strike while the iron is hot'. What's more, if we wait longer, won't we be more likely to have forgotten the information? This is actually true. However, by waiting until the information is less well remembered, the later study session has more of a benefit. It's rather like waiting to paint a second coat of paint on a wall—there's no point in starting until the previous coat has dried.

A useful exploration of the spacing effect by psychologist Melody Wiseheart used flashcards to present learners with 32 obscure trivia questions, along the lines of 'what European nation consumes the most spicy Mexican food?' (the answer was Norway!). After an initial study session, learners were given a chance to restudy the information a number of days later—sometimes the gap between study and restudy was as long as 3.5 months. For others, restudy took place after just a few minutes. In total, hundreds of learners took part in the research.

Later (sometimes as much as a year later), the participants were tested. These timescales are very relevant to school and college learning, where you may well study something in September and be tested on it in May, for example. Findings showed that in general, the benefits of a delay between study and restudy increased up until a point, after which they started to decline again.[20] For a test that took place a year later, a gap between study and restudy of around 20 days was best, though this 'optimal' gap was shorter if the test took place sooner after the second study session. In other words, the longer you want to remember something, the more valuable it is to space study sessions out further apart. However the researchers stated, "*although there are costs to using a gap that is longer than the optimal value, these costs are much smaller than the costs of using too short a gap*" (p. 1101). In other words, it is always wasteful and inefficient to study something again too soon.

In practical terms, it's worth noting that the original study session had involved learners practicing until they got all of the flashcards right, and then stopping (in other words, mastery had been achieved but there was no overlearning—see Chapter 2). Spacing is unlikely to be helpful if mastery has *not* been achieved—instead, learning on a topic should continue until you have fully mastered the material. This will depend on you, as well as on the difficulty of the topic you are studying. Although your independent study is the second time you have learned the material—as you have already looked at it in class or in your reading—it's probably going to be the first time you have achieved mastery (unless you did a *lot* of practice during a lesson).

Overall then, you need to judge how good your knowledge is now, and time a delay before restudy accordingly. If you were to make flashcards on the day of (or even during) a lesson/lecture, how many would you get right two days later? How about a month later? If you would get them all right, it's too soon to do further study. As soon as forgetting starts to have a major impact, it's time to restudy.

Applying the spacing effect

In practical terms, the spacing effect presents a trade-off between the benefit of a delay and the costs of forgetting. Imagine that you have 20 days until your exam. You can study the material today, and then one more time. When should you do it? According to this effect, you don't want to do this second study session too soon after the initial one, as you won't benefit from spacing. On the other hand, you don't want to leave it too late, both because forgetting will increase, and because you clearly can't restudy everything in the day or two before the exam. Therefore, a second session towards the mid-point of the remaining time would make sense.

However, as mentioned in the previous section, the scientific best time for restudy depends on a lot of factors, and it's unfortunately therefore not possible to say "*space your study by x days*" and have it always be the right choice. We can at least say that once mastery has been achieved, spacing your restudy will always be an improvement compared to doing it immediately or very soon. The following simple guidelines—based on my own spacing effect research as well as my years as a teacher and exam marker—show you how to put this into practice.

Firstly, it is highly likely that information has not been learned to mastery level after a single class or lecture. If you have followed the advice in Chapter 4, you have taken steps to develop a comprehensive set of notes without taking a huge amount of time over this process. One of the reasons for this advice is that your time is much better spent consolidating this learning after class, using retrieval practice.

Secondly, many students tend to consolidate/restudy too soon. Whether this involves homework or reading over notes, it's common to do follow-up work in the day or two after an initial class. Here, it's actually the disorganised students who have the advantage! Consolidating the material would be best left until a period of time has passed.

Thirdly, most students don't restudy at all between the initial lesson/homework period and the exam. Therefore even if something is learned well at that initial stage, a harmful amount of forgetting will occur before the exam. Have you ever got to exam time and looked over your notes, and found that you don't even remember studying it the first time around, never mind remembering the details? To avoid this happening, you need to schedule a revision session midway between these points, for example around a month after the initial study.

Fourthly, if you have a midterm/mock/prelim exam, there is a tendency not to take it seriously. This is a mistake, because such exams are often really well-timed in terms of spacing (by accident rather than design, but let's make the most of it!).

For example, if the initial learning took place in September, you scheduled in a review in October, then a midterm/mock in January or February would be a really good time for the next study session for an exam that takes place in early summer. Such a schedule will make everything much easier when that exam comes around.

Interleaving

Interleaving is a popular but widely misunderstood strategy. Part of the reason for this is that the term applies to two different things—initial learning, and practice/revision. Here we will focus just on practice.

Interleaved practice means that the order of items that you practice is shuffled, such that different types of item appear side by side. So for example, rather than studying and testing yourself just on quotes by Shakespeare, you might mix up flashcards showing quotes from several plays by different authors. It may sound like a recipe for confusion, but in fact interleaved practice helps you to notice differences between items[21] leading to better recall as well as better recognition of similar new items (i.e. it helps with transfer—see Chapter 3).

It will immediately occur to you that revision flashcards are easy to shuffle and thereby interleave. A word of caution, though—the research has tended to only show a benefit of interleaving items that are similar and therefore easily confused.[22] This means that it would be an advantage to interleave flashcards from the same topic, or perhaps even the whole subject. However, if topics were entirely unrelated, interleaving would not have the same advantage, because the items are too different. Nobody is going to mix up a Shakespeare quote with a chemical formula, for example. In this scenario, it would be best to keep similar items together, making it easy to make meaningful connections between them.

A practical guideline, then, is to freely shuffle cards within courses or topics (this may happen accidentally, as you work through them), but if you study different school or university subjects, keep the bundles of cards for these subjects separate.

An additional benefit of interleaved practice is that it is more unpredictable, and therefore better preparation for a test or exam. Do you remember how in Chapter 2, I described the weakness of overlearning a set of very similar maths questions? The same research team led by Doug Rohrer has found that interleaving different sorts of maths questions can pay dividends. One reason for this, they argue, is that by seeing practice questions in an unpredictable order, it's much harder to know what strategy is required at the outset[23] (something that is immediately obvious if you practice a page of the same sort of questions).

Further considerations when scheduling

Another implication of the spacing effect is that it would make sense to divide topics up, so that they are studied in several short bursts rather than one long session. Imagine again that you have an exam that is in 20 days' time, and let's say there are 10 topics to cover. That averages out as two days per topic, so it might be natural to study one topic for the first two days, then the 2nd topic on days three and four, and so on. However, the spacing effect tells us that it would be much more effective to space all ten topics out, rather than covering each in a single block. This could mean studying each one to mastery over a few hours, and then not coming back to it until at least a couple of days later. With such a method, you might actually get well-earned days off, too (indeed, the spacing effect is a great excuse for taking more breaks!).

How does this link to interleaving? Well, as the main benefit of interleaving is allowing you to contrast individual items and making this practice unpredictable, there is no particular reason to mix up entire topics within one day. Doing so would be hard to keep track of, meaning that you might fail to study some parts of your course. So it's fine to focus on a particular subject or topic during a day—but do interleave flashcards and concepts within that topic, and don't forget to return to the same topic on a future day in order to benefit from spacing.

Retrieval practice can be combined very well with the spacing effect. As you build up your stock of key ideas/terms and quotes on flashcards, these can be used to test yourself every so often. The additional effort of preparing a good set of material throughout your course will now start to pay off. As a general rule, wait long enough so that the material on the flashcards becomes hard to remember—if you can remember it all easily from the last session, you are restudying too soon (how long this takes this will depend on both you and the difficulty of the topic). It may feel quite uncomfortable to wait until it becomes harder to remember the material, but the extra effort needed to answer questions during well-spaced study sessions will really boost your learning.

Review questions

1. Does the spacing effect suggest that we should study again soon after an initial study session, or wait for a while?

2. What must be done in order to see the benefits of a delay before restudy?
3. What's the best way to interleave the concepts on your flashcards?

7

Focus and passion

How important is attention to the learning process?
What steps can I take to boost concentration?
How does emotion play a role in learning?

G ood strategies are important, but they can't take the place of motivation. Have you ever started a project with great enthusiasm, forcing yourself through difficulties, only to run out of steam after a few days or weeks?

When studying too, you are likely to struggle for motivation over the longer term. The fact that you'd like to gain a top grade might not be enough by itself to motivate you to revise on a cold winter's night, with a summer exam many months away.

Perhaps when you do study, you find that nothing is going in, or that you tend to get caught up with doodling or daydreaming, and waste hours of study time to little benefit? This chapter will tackle these issues.

Attention

According to British psychologist Alan Baddeley, attention is the central component of working memory, allowing all other processes to take place.[24] If you don't pay attention to something and focus on it, then the information will quickly fade and be forgotten.

You have probably had the experience of reading a book, only to realise that although your eyes were following the words, you were actually thinking about something else. And how much from the page could you remember? Nothing, is the answer. Similarly, if you don't pay attention when studying from items such as flashcards or concept maps, the material has no chance of entering your memory. This is why multi-tasking is such a bad idea. It is best to study with as few distractions as possible—alone, and with the TV off, and definitely not combining study with socialising. If possible, switch off your phone and disconnect your wi-fi for a period of time.

A related issue to address is daydreaming, or *mind-wandering* as it's technically called (because it has nothing to do with dreams, and needn't happen during the day!). Mind-wandering may happen during reading, or during a lecture. It can even happen mid-conversation. The definition of mind-wandering is that the mind is occupied by internal thoughts rather than by external stimulation or activity.[25]

It's important to recognise that mind-wandering is normal—it's common during any class or study session, and we probably can't get rid of it entirely. It does link to how interesting and challenging something is; mind-wandering happens more if something is too easy.

Mind-wandering may actually have some benefits—it appears to link to creativity and the drive to form meaningful associations, meaning that time spent staring out of a window mid-task may not be entirely wasted! However, it remains the case that if you are not focusing attention on the task at hand, key information will not be entering your long-term memory.

Concentration

Another important implication of what we know about attention and mind-wandering is that it is hard to focus on study for a long period of time. Generally, we can pay attention well at the start of a study session, but after a few minutes our attention tends to wane, unless we find the topic especially fascinating. Imagine listening to a fairly dry talk or lecture—how long could you concentrate for? Ten minutes? Twenty? You may well find that this varies, and that you can either focus for less time or more time than your peers (this variation may be due to you finding the topic easier or more interesting than they do).

Some people like to doodle (draw unplanned, simple patterns or sketches) as they listen, and this may not be a bad thing at all for concentration. An interesting research study by British psychologist Jackie Andrade found that when listening to information over the phone, people remembered 29% more information if they doodled than if they did not.[26] This is a curious and unusual case of multi-tasking being beneficial, compared to focusing on a single task. Why? Recall that multi-tasking is problematic because it divides our limited attention or uses the same part of working memory (e.g. verbal working memory). Because doodling is a relatively unconscious and automatic process, it doesn't use up a significant amount of attention (the same applies to other mostly unconscious processes such as scratching an itch). It's also a visual process, so doesn't interfere with the verbal working memory needed to listen during a class.

Furthermore, we know that the mind tends to wander, leading to reduced concentration. It may be that doodling, or another relatively automatic physical processes (fiddling with a toy, perhaps) helps to maintain a level of concentration on our surroundings during times when the mind would otherwise wander. So go ahead and doodle!

This finding only applies to really automatic, absent-minded doodling, though—if you are doing proper drawing/art work, this will use up the limited amount of attention available to your working memory, and therefore reduce how much information you can take in.

Perceptive readers might wonder if doodling might be a form of dual coding; this is likely only to be the case if the doodle matches what is listened to. If so, and the doodles are essentially drawings of the subject matter, they could certainly be beneficial to memory. This idea has also been investigated by researchers—in a 2017 study, Jeffrey Wammes and colleagues found that drawn notes led to superior recall relative to written notes.[27] These were proper drawings, though, sketches of the concepts from a class, rather than absent-minded doodles.

Doodling is also more likely to interfere with visual working memory during visual tasks, so it may be best avoided during lectures in subjects such as engineering or architecture, or indeed any area where visualising a new concept is important.

When it comes to your own self-paced revision it is unlikely that you will get so bored that you need to doodle midway through, and if you do, you should probably take a break. I think that students often try to study for too long at a time, and their 'study sessions' often descend into chatting, internet browsing and other distractions. More breaks help, but these can often be overly long, leading to a lack of study progress!

How long you can focus for at a time can be self-tested (see Chapter 10), and this information can guide the approximate duration of your study sessions. Build in frequent breaks—but make the breaks very short (a few minutes can be enough) so that you are not wasting a lot of time overall. The *pomodoro technique* is a system which is based on this idea. According to the technique, work or study should take place in blocks of 25 minutes, each followed by five minute breaks. After every fourth session, you take a longer break. The technique gets its name from the tomato-shaped kitchen timers—'pomodoro' is Italian for tomato—though of course a phone timer could be used (there are also many pomodoro technique apps). The breaks could include walking to another room to stretch your legs, getting a drink, or doing a very brief bout of exercise. One experiment found that students who were given three five-minute exercise breaks during a lecture learned better and experienced less mind-wandering compared to breaks playing a computer game, or no break at all.[28]

Overall then, short, focused sessions using active study techniques (as described in the previous chapters) are the best approach with short active breaks in between times.

Emotional engagement

As mentioned above, it's harder to concentrate on a difficult or dry lecture. Some things are much easier than others to focus on, and as noted earlier in this book, learning actively can be as much about what is going on internally (being mentally active) as what you are doing externally.

It's hard to hack your emotional engagement with a subject—we generally like some subjects and dislike others (and I'd certainly recommend picking subjects that you find interesting). But you can at least find aspects of the subject that you like, and focus on those. Imagine, for example, you are studying Psychology and you want to be a teacher. You could take almost any topic in psychology and link it to your chosen career: memory (obviously!), intelligence, personality (of teachers and students), obedience (classroom behaviour), stress (of teachers, as well as how it affects learning), prejudice (how to reduce it in the classroom)...the list goes on.

Another great way to boost your emotional engagement is to read around the subject. Recommendations from your teacher/lecturer would be a good place to start if you are not otherwise sure. There are some incredible popular science books in every subject conceivable. Take *Sophie's World* by Jostein Gardner for Philosophy, for example, or *Guns, Germs & Steel* by Jared Diamond for Human Geography. These sorts of books are as engaging as a novel, easy to read, and motivating. They also help to develop a lot of background schema knowledge which can be helpful when learning about new concepts.

Finally, emotion in learning is partly linked to identity. People are more motivated and learn better if the view a subject as fitting their perception of who they are as a person. Despite the fact that girls tend to do well at STEM subjects during the early years of school (indeed, girls outperform boys across the academic spectrum at primary/elementary school for a variety of reasons), relatively few female adolescents see STEM subjects as being 'a girl thing'.[29] For this reason, they are less likely to choose these subjects, potentially reducing their chances of later advancing to highly-paid science and engineering careers. So if you still have some key choices ahead of you, it's worth taking some time to reflect on whether you are choosing subjects because it is really your sort of thing, or just because that is the expectation of peers, teachers or parents.

Review questions

1. Do we need to pay attention when learning?
2. When might doodling be helpful?
3. When using the pomodoro technique, how long are the study sessions and how long are the breaks?

8

Exam preparation

Is it worth taking the time to plan an answer?
What's a scenario question?
What are command terms?

The age-old invocation to students is to *answer the question.* This is vital. In my own exam-marking experience, I have seen good quality answers (in the sense of being accurate and full of detail) awarded zero marks if they had failed to address what was actually being asked.

This may seem very pedantic, but one valid reason behind it is to discourage students from memorising an answer during revision and then simply writing it down in the exam, regardless of what's in the exam paper. There is also an argument that it prepares learners for the real world—in a job, workers need to produce what they've been asked for (e.g. a report, article or web copy), and not write anything they feel like.

Beyond the practice of sticking to the question, this chapter looks at several key things that can be learned from good use of practice exam materials.

Getting the right materials

Let's assume that you have taken the time to establish good sets of Cornell-style study notes, taken accurate summary notes from your textbook(s), and made comprehensive and accurate flashcards and concept maps (see Chapter 4). Well done! You're well set to prepare for the exam.

Next, you need to find past papers/practice papers. They do exist. As a teacher myself, I will do my best to accommodate a student who asks for extra practice questions, even if it just means pointing them in the direction of revision books. Many textbooks include entire practice exams. For some major national exams (e.g. SATs, A-Levels or AP exams), questions are widely available online. With university modules it may be down to the institution or lecturer as to whether they release past papers or not, but it doesn't hurt to ask.

Don't forget to get hold of the rubric/marking instructions too, if at all possible. Unfortunately, these are not always available, and if they are, they are often phrased in a way that makes little sense to students. The reason for this is that they are not aimed at you—they are a guide for markers. Nevertheless, with some practice, you can get an idea of what will or will not be awarded marks. Again, no teacher worthy of their position will refuse to give their students reasonable advice on what exam markers will be looking for, even if they cannot release practice papers.

Planning

Planning should be undertaken for any longer exam question (of course, it's not necessary for multiple choice or very short answers). It is a neglected area in exams, not least due to the time constraints. In contrast to the careful plans and drafts that characterise term papers and reports, exam answers tend to be written in a rush with little or no planning. Taking 5% of the exam time at the start to read questions carefully and plan the answers could be time very well spent.

The order in which you tackle questions can also (usually) be planned. Some teachers advise doing your best question (the one you feel most confident in) first, followed by your worst one. This gets you off to a positive start, and still allows you to tackle the hardest question before you get tired.

It continues to surprise me how few students plan out the essays that are likely to come up in their exam. Granted, writing a practice essay is quite time consuming. But it is very beneficial—especially if there are a limited number of possible questions that could come up. As with any skill, essay writing gets quicker with practice. Practice essays are also a good opportunity to get teacher feedback. Over the course of a year, depending on your overall workload, it may be possible to build up a file of the most common essays, get feedback, and then rewrite them in accordance with this feedback (although don't put yourself under too much pressure—you shouldn't compromise on getting good sleep and sufficient breaks). At the very least, it would be beneficial to have thought about the most common essay questions and mentally planned them out (see also Chapter 9 for advice for the run up to an exam).

Scenario questions

These days, many exams feature scenario questions—ones where you have to comment on or respond to a previously-unseen scenario, rather than simply answering a question.

From the point of view of the people who set exams, this forces students to show transfer (the ability to apply learned information to a new context—see Chapter 3), and avoids encouraging memorisation. Of course, you now know that memory is an integral part of learning, but teachers also want learners to remember things in a way that is flexible and can be used in the future, not just reciting a pre-written answer word for word. Similar questions also feature in university entrance tests or interviews.

It's very important to fully engage with a scenario, rather than just picking out a few details and sprinkling them into an otherwise prepared answer. Doing so will show a marker that you have good reading and analysis skills, and may get credit in itself, as well as making your answer more coherent.

One of the best ways to prepare for scenario questions is to do a lot of reading of similar scenarios in the real world. For example, perhaps there are blogs about your subject where people talk about theories and how they have been applied. Alternatively, you could post a question on social media, asking for examples of how people have used (your choice of theory) in the real world.

Command terms and high-level skills

Sometimes exams are very strict about what information they are looking for, and it is vital that you pay close attention to the first word of the question/directive, for example "Describe..." or "Evaluate...". In my own experience as a marker, it was not uncommon for answers to be given zero marks if they described something when they had been asked to evaluate, and so forth.

A related issue is that some skills are considered to be better or more important than others. Describing and explaining are typically seen as more basic skills than the likes of applying and evaluating. This idea is not without its critics, but it remains the case that many courses value these 'high-level skills', and that you can therefore acquire more credit in exams for demonstrating them in your answers.

A good starting place for any evaluation question is to simply ask what's good and bad about the concept that's being discussed. However, you may need to take this further by explaining why it's a good or a bad thing. What's the consequence of a particular advantage or flaw? What would happen if that consequence were to occur? For example:

> *'A limitation of fracking for oil is that it can cause pollution to the local water supply. While this might be manageable on a small scale, a large amount of fracking in a particular location could cause enough pollution to affect the supplies of drinking water to farms and communities. The consequence of this could be increased incidence of health problems...'*

Analysis is a very subject-specific skill, but as a general rule, analysing something means taking it apart, explaining each part, and discussing how the parts work together and why they are the way they are. An analysis of a research study, for example, could involve explaining its aims and methodology, how it was a step forward from previous research, why a particular group of research participants were used, and so forth. An analysis of a law could involve explaining the different parts of the law, what each sets out to do, and what the reasoning behind it is.

Given the way these skills differ across subjects and exams, this is an area where it's important to take specific advice from your teacher and (where applicable) your textbook.

Walking-talking mocks

A 'walking-talking mock' is a strategy used in some high schools in England, but which can be applied to other contexts. It involves a teacher going through an exam question and 'walking students through' (i.e. demonstrating) the steps to answering the question. It's particularly useful for tricky questions, where learners are likely to go down the wrong track or misread a question. The key thing is that learners are not writing practice answers, but are being given a step by step demonstration. This usually involves showing steps of the answer on a screen.

If your class doesn't currently feature this, you could suggest it to your teacher. Alternatively, you could establish a group discussion with classmates where you collectively talk through (rather than answer) a past paper, or start a similar discussion on an online student forum (or virtual learning environment, if your institution has one).

Mnemonics

When discussing study skills, the first thing that comes to mind for many students is *mnemonics*—a range of memory tricks used to help remember key information. Typically mnemonics make use of rhymes, phrases, or visualisation in order to prompt memory of key details. Sometimes these help us to remember the order of a set of items.

For example, the phrase 'Richard Of York Gave Battle In Vain' helps us to remember the letters ROYGBIV, the first initials of the colours of the visible spectrum/rainbow. The phrase allows us to remember that orange comes in between red and yellow; this order is supported by the fact that the words wouldn't make sense in a different order.

In other cases, the order might not matter much, but there is a defined set of information and you can use the same strategy to avoid missing anything vital. For example: to remember the names of the carpal bones (bones of the human wrist), many medical students use a mnemonic such as 'Sally Left The Party To Take Cathy Home' to prompt recall of 'scaphoid, lunate, triquetrum, pisiform, trapezium, trapezoid, capitate, hamate', as they share their first letters with the words of the phrase.

Sometimes there is a bit of both, such as when a phrase is used to remember both the letters and order of letters for the correct way to spell a word. For example: the spelling of 'necessary' using the phrase 'Never Eat Cheese, Eat Sausage Sandwiches And Remain Young'.

Visual images are also powerful. A difficult-to-remember piece of terminology could be remembered by thinking of one or more words that it sounds like, and then connecting this visually with the item you are trying to remember. For example: an old (pre-electric) miner's lamp was called a Davy lamp. You might try to remember this by picturing a person you know called Dave/David down a mine. Better still, picture him *falling* down a mine, as this is a more dynamic visual image.

These techniques are certainly useful. However, the reason I have left them until (almost) the end of this book is that they are not really about learning—they are about prompting recall of things that you have already learned. The phrase about 'Sally left the party...' is useless to someone who hasn't already learned the names of the carpal bones.

In addition, it's hard to generate enough visual images—and

to make each distinctive enough—for it to make a major impact on learning overall. Such images also tend to be short lived in memory.[30] These are therefore best left for items that are still proving difficult during the later stages of revision, such as hard-to-remember terminology or tricky foreign language vocabulary. Over time, the image may be forgotten, but repeated retrieval and use means that the item itself will not be.

It's important to understand that mnemonics are not a short-cut, and they can't replace learning. However, they can help to support recall of specific difficult areas, especially under the stress of exam conditions. They are particularly useful for organising information, especially when the order is important, and as a prompt to aid recall of previously studied information.

Sleep

Let's not forget the importance of sleep to the learning process. Did you know that memories are consolidated during sleep? Sleep seems to be essential for turning temporary information in LTM into permanent memory traces. Sleep also seems to play a role in reorganising memory, it may affect problem solving and creativity, and it's vital for the brain to repair itself and replenish energy and other chemicals in our neurons, clearing out toxins simultaneously. Really, it's not optional—particularly for students!

An interesting study by American sleep researchers Amy Wolfson and Mary Carskadon found that adolescents who got more sleep and whose sleep was more regular (in the sense of getting a similar amount each day, rather than catching up at weekends) tended to get higher grades at school than their peers with worse sleep habits. The latter group also tended to be moodier, and to feel sleepier at school. It's hard to know whether sleep was the only factor in this difference in grades, but it certainly fits with a hypothesis that poor sleep harms concentration and memory.

Of course, sleep is not an easy thing to modify, as anyone with insomnia will tell you. If you are in your teens or early 20s, it may be useful to know that the body clock naturally shifts later in your age group, so tending to lie in bed later and stay up into the early hours of the morning is not laziness—it's written in your genes. Similarly, some people (around 25% of us) are naturally 'night owls', meaning that they tend to work better later in the day.

Daniel Pink's 2018 book, 'When: The Scientific Secrets of Perfect Timing' shows that there is more still to the body clock. For night owls, as well as for morning people ('larks') and anyone in between, there tends to be a slump time in the early afternoon. This is the worst time to do any productive work or things that require concentration, and could instead be used for more routine tasks like cleaning or doing some exercise.

When it comes to getting a good night sleep, a routine is helpful—though not always compatible with the student lifestyle. Most people can cope with having a night or two per week where you stay up later, as long as you retain a reasonable level of routine the rest of the time. Avoid doing things that mess with your body clock, like staying in a darkened room during the day, or staring at a screen all evening. And of course, caffeine and other stimulants can keep you awake, so confine the strong coffees to the afternoon or earlier.

Interestingly, naps can have similar benefits to a night's sleep in terms of memory. From this point of view, napping could be a partial solution for those of us who find it hard to get 7–8 hours of sleep per night. It's important not to nap too late in the day—experts tend to recommend no later than 4pm, in order to avoid making it harder to get to sleep at night. So a nap could be another use for that early-afternoon slump (as some cultures around the world have been doing for years).

Review questions

1. What kind of learning do scenario questions aim to test?
2. Give an example of a command word that could be used in an exam question, and explain why it's important to pay attention to these.
3. What are mnemonics more useful for—learning information, or prompting recall?
4. Name one effect of sleep.

9

Just before your exam

How should I study with a week or two to go?
How should I study on the last day before my exam?

As mentioned earlier, spacing out your study is best over the long term, but if time is very limited, a degree of cramming can be helpful.

Prioritising is also essential. You can't restudy the entire course content in a day, or even a fortnight. Prioritising could involve an analysis of which questions feature most prominently on the exam. It involves spending more time on items which are most likely to have a high payoff, and paying less attention to those which are more of a long-shot (without skipping them entirely).

The best advice will vary depending on how soon your exam is, so the following guidance considers the issue from the perspective of having a week or two to go, or just 24 hours until your test/exam. It applies to students who have left their work a bit too late, but also to those who simply want to know how to spend those last few days as productively as possible. Given that this is advice for when you are most pushed for time, this chapter does not feature review questions!

If you have a week or two to go

Your exam is close, so it's time to really focus. There's no room for procrastination, but you do still have enough time (if you use it well) to seriously upgrade your level of detailed knowledge as well as your exam technique.

The first thing you should do is to make sure you have everything you need. This includes your textbook(s), classroom notes and concept maps, set of flashcards, your own summaries from your reading, and any available past papers or lists of practice questions. If you haven't been making revision flashcards all year, it's too time consuming to start now—either find some online via a site like Quizlet.com (there's a good chance that previous students from your course have made theirs freely available), or make do with testing yourself on items from the glossary of your textbook, or a similar list of key terms.

Regarding where to work, you don't need to have a single study space, but at least have an idea of where you are going to get your revision done—somewhere quiet where you have a good amount of space and can spread out your books and plug in your laptop. Where do you work best? ('At a friend's house' is the wrong answer!). Interestingly, psychologists agree that it's worth dividing your study between several places, to avoid the memories becoming too context-specific.[31]

Another valuable thing to do with at least a week (or preferably a fortnight) to go is to run through all of your revision flashcards. This will help to refresh detailed knowledge ahead of the remainder of your study sessions. Test yourself until you get each concept right at least once.

Next, it's time to take a realistic look at how much time you have left for revision. Sketch a rough timetable which includes each study session and break. This should focus around identifying short slots of time—around an hour is fine (the pomodoro technique, where you study in 25 minute bursts, is ideal for a day but probably too intensive to do for a whole fortnight). One option at this stage is to follow your normal weekly school or university timetable, if you have one—this is an already-learned structure which will be easier to stick to than a brand new timetable that you have only just invented. For example, if you normally have classes between 9 a.m. and 3 p.m. with a one-hour lunch break, this will be easy to remember as a study schedule. If you want to study in the evening in addition, this is a good time to work on practice essays.

Overall, you should probably aim to fit in around five hour-long sessions per day on average. For most people there's little point in trying to do much more than this—you'll just burn out. Really long study sessions also tend not to be very productive, especially if they are interspersed with chatting with friends, listening to music, or checking social media (in fact, it's probably best to confine all your socialising, with family or friends, to a certain time of the day, e.g. at the end of the day when your work is done).

Now, allocate each topic or subtopic to a session. For example if your course had eight topics and each of these had three subtopics, then you have 24 subtopics to divide between the available study sessions. According to the advice above, you should have 70 sessions available across 14 days, so each subtopic can be allocated more than once. That's fine—it means that you'll go back to each area of the course after a few days and study it again, consolidating what you have already done and benefiting from the spacing effect. However, keep the last couple of days of your plan clear, both as a contingency in case of illness, and to allow time for last minute preparation (see the next section). In addition, you must take proper breaks, whether whole days or the occasional afternoon/morning—it's your choice. This probably means that you will have more like 50 one-hour study sessions over a fortnight.

What should you actually do during each study session? One of the best things at this stage is to rewrite your concept maps from memory to check that you still remember how topics fit together, and don't have any gaps in your overall understanding (see Chapter 4). It's really important to do this from memory, not by copying!

Another very valuable task is to work through your textbook or your own detailed written summaries (or both), checking your level of recall and understanding. As discussed in Chapter 2, passive re-reading is an ineffective study strategy, so instead, you should aim to use a strategy called *elaborative interrogation*. This means asking questions as you go through each part of the text, in particular, asking yourself 'why' questions—combining the benefits of elaborated examples, and the high-level skills discussed in the previous chapter. This is a useful technique at any stage of your studies but particularly now during revision, because the technique has been shown to work better after schema knowledge has been developed.[32] In addition, if you followed the suggestion about using Cornell notes system (see Chapter 4), you should already have key questions written down one side of your classroom notes.

Writing a concept map plus working through the reading may well take a couple of study sessions, or even more. How does your rate of study compare with how many topics/subtopics you have to cover? The time you have left is fixed, so if you are going too fast or too slow, you can make some adjustments now. If you have time to tackle a third or fourth session on each subtopic, then move on to writing out full exam-style questions—it is always valuable to practice these, and you are likely to be ready to do well in them having already worked through the content in detail. Again, a more active task and one that uses retrieval is preferable, so even if you have already written out practice essays during the year, it's useful to rewrite one from memory rather than to read through your previous attempts.

If you come across areas where you feel confused, there may still be enough time to get some help from your teacher or lecturer at this stage. However, as time ticks down and you find yourself with only a few days left, don't spend the time travelling in to university or school (which would use up valuable time that could be spent studying). Instead, make contact by email; it's not unreasonable to send a list of queries with a few days still to go—most teachers will be happy to address these (but don't expect them to mark essays in the last few days).

Overall, high priorities with one or two weeks to go include:
- Ensuring you have all of your key materials including past papers.
- Running through key content using flashcards.
- Planning your remaining time, dividing days into around five short study sessions that follow your usual timetable.
- Allocating subtopics to each study session, covering every topic twice or more but allowing for days/afternoons off.
- Moving on to writing practice questions.
- Making contact with your teacher by email if there are areas of particular difficulty.

The final day

Clearly having only a day or two to go until your exam is not ideal, but at some point, we all get to the stage where there is very little time left. Whether you have been working systematically through your learning and revision all year or have left it all a bit too late, there are still several important things that you can do at this stage. The following applies to the final day before the exam and will be expressed as such, though these tasks would be best begun with two days to go.

Your main focus should be on dividing up the available study time over the final day(s) into short, focused blocks of around 25 minutes, with <u>short</u> breaks in between (i.e. using the pomodoro technique—see Chapter 7). Actually write this schedule down, with the timings of each study session—doing so will only take a few minutes, and the external written list of times will help you to stick to the plan (as will setting a countdown timer on your phone for each session!). Allow a decent amount of time for meal breaks, though. And don't plan on either getting an early night or staying up late—neither of these things will help.

Make sure your study space is comfortable and quiet, that you have water and snacks to hand, and use the five-minute breaks in between sessions to get a bit of exercise (even just walking outside for some fresh air and back again).

You can't relearn your course in a day, but you can familiarise yourself with the exam format in that time. From my own teaching experience, I feel that exam technique can make as much as a 10% difference to a student's eventual grade. Therefore, even with such a short time to go, it's worth using the first of your remaining study sessions to look over the format of the exam (if that information is available), and check that you know all of the key details: how long the exam paper is, how many marks each section is worth, what is mandatory and what is optional, and so on. Take notes of these details as you go, and look over them all one more time just before the exam starts. Later in the day you will be doing exam practice (see below), which will consolidate this new understanding (it's also worth double checking *where and when* the exam is, if you're not sure).

For your remaining morning study sessions, you should focus on rapid-fire retrieval of key terms and concept knowledge. For all types of exam, it's going to be really valuable to work through these key terms and test yourself. Granted, this is cramming, and not the best way to learn over the long-term, but with a day to go it's your most effective option, and will result in some real gains (in contrast to passive activities such as re-reading class notes or highlighting textbook chapters). The main focus should be testing yourself using flashcards, practice questions, or other sets of course content (as noted above, you may be able to find ready-made sets of flashcards online if you haven't prepared any).

In each study session, therefore, work through a set of flash-cards or multiple choice questions until you get all of the answers right. One excellent option would be to work through all of your flashcards in the morning (shuffle them all together, to gain the benefits of interleaved practice; see Chapter 6) and then move on to practicing specific exam-style questions in the afternoon.

As you get the answer to each flashcard correct, put it to one side, so that you have a gradually decreasing bundle left in your hands. Keep going until you have got every answer correct at least once. With terms and definitions, it is a good idea to start with the definitions (i.e. recalling the terms) and then switching the sides of the cards in order to do the more challenging task of remembering the definitions from looking at the term. This means you will go through all of them again, retrieving key information from memory once more.

Moving onto exam practice later in the day, let's focus first on exam papers which are made up partly or entirely of short-answer or multiple-choice questions. You should hopefully now be in a position to answer such questions quickly and confidently, having just revised the key terms that morning. Do so without referring to your notes, to ensure that you are actively drawing on memory (yes, it may feel uncomfortable, but it's much more beneficial!).

Check through all your answers (assuming answers are freely available; if unavailable, contact a friend or use Google). If there were any that you found a struggle to answer, check these particularly carefully—you will learn a lot from tackling the gaps, for if the same question comes up in tomorrow's exam, your revision session will be recent enough in mind that you should have a clear episodic memory of struggling with the question and then looking up the answer. There may be a few areas that you still really struggle with even after going through practice questions, and for these it would be worth creating verbal or visual mnemonics (see Chapter 8).

For exam papers that involve writing extended answers, take a few minutes at the start of each of the afternoon's short study sessions to look at practice questions/past paper questions on that topic, paying attention to the command term used (e.g. describe, evaluate). This can make a major difference to the outcome, and it's worth noting which ones come up most often. If you don't already have a set of practice questions, it's probably too late to get teacher advice on this, but use social media to ask your classmates—the chances are, someone has already compiled a list and will be willing to share it with you. Again, answering these questions is most valuable without referring to your notes, but do check your answers at the end of the study session.

If you're going to be dealing with full-length essay questions then clearly you won't have time to write a practice answer to every possible question in a single afternoon. However, you can pick some of the most likely ones to come up, ensuring that you are tackling every topic or subtopic at some point. In each study session, you should instead write a detailed plan that lists what will go into your answer, dividing the essay up paragraph by paragraph. If available, refer to model answers, considering details such how they set out an introduction, how many paragraphs they have, how long they are overall in terms of word count, and how much detail is given in the supporting evidence used.

Overall, high priorities with a day to go include:

- Ensuring that you are clear on the format of the exam
- A final run-though of key terms and concepts, ideally testing yourself on flashcards.
- Doing practice exam questions and/or detailed essay plans.
- A degree of prioritising among possible topics.

10

Investigating your own learning

How can you best decide which techniques to use, and when?
If you were going to investigate your own learning, what would you compare, and what factors would you have to keep constant?

The previous sections have explained the current scientific understanding of human memory and what it implies for learning and revision. However, as with anything in science, the context can make a big difference to how processes work. It will be valuable to put the principles to the test throughout the course of your own learning.

This chapter will guide you to systematically compare your own performance with and without these techniques, helping you to select the ones that make the biggest difference in your context and that you find motivating, and to make evidence-based decisions about exactly how to apply them.

Why study your own learning?

A number of points raised in the book so far—such as the futility of re-reading, or the benefits of spacing and retrieval practice—have been described as counterintuitive, meaning that it's not immediately obvious whether they would (or wouldn't) help.

This is because people have flawed *metacognition*—a term meaning our ability to think about our own thinking. It is common to hear students say things like "I know this works for me". But a large body of research has shown that students believe that flawed strategies do work, and fail to appreciate the benefits of learning strategies backed by science (and that this remains true even if people are given a chance to try other strategies themselves).

The good news is that flawed metacognition is not your fault—like other mistaken beliefs, you have picked up ideas about learning from more experienced people in your life, and assumed that what they were saying was true. Like many areas of life, we tend to take the word of people around us (or from the media) without fact-checking everything that they say.

However, the bad news is that flawed metacognition is your problem. If you don't take action and do something about it, you will continue to waste time on flawed strategies and be susceptible to future myths and misconceptions that you hear. It's time for a more sceptical, evidence-based approach to learning.

Advice such as the ideas presented this book can only go so far. I can tell you what works in general, but some aspects will be specific to your preferences and the material you are studying. People read at different speeds, have their own unique sets of prior knowledge, and have different strengths and weaknesses in terms of concentration and working memory. Investigating your learning will allow you to tailor your study strategies to fit your own particular needs.

A simple experiment

Normally experiments are conducted on groups of people, but some of the earliest psychology experiments into learning and memory were conducted on a single person. In the late 1800s, German researcher Hermann Ebbinghaus conducted a series of experiments on himself, testing his own short-term and long-term memory, and making early discoveries (including the spacing effect) that still prove useful today. You can take a leaf from Ebbinghaus's book by experimenting on your own learning.

A simple experiment can involve comparing one strategy with another in a way that holds every other variable constant (that is, it's a 'fair test'). This is actually quite difficult to do, because obviously you can't study the same material using two strategies simultaneously, and if you study using first one and then the other strategy, then the comparison is no longer fair and equal (because you have already practiced the material once).

It's therefore best to try techniques on two different but equally-matched sets of study materials, while trying to keep everything else as constant as possible. A good way to do this would be to randomly divide a large set of flashcards into two piles, in the same way that you would shuffle and deal a deck of cards. Alternatively, two textbook chapters could be used if you are confident that they are pretty equal in difficulty (the course teacher could be asked for advice on this). A third option—ideal for comparing note-taking strategies—would be to compare taking notes in two separate classes on the same course, each lasting the same length of time.

Having established your set of materials, have a try at completing these study sessions in a way that allows you to find out about the effect of one key change—such as comparing two forms of note taking, or studying with and without summarising the concept—while keeping everything else equal as far as possible. Things to keep as constant as possible could include the time of day, the food and drink you consume (especially caffeine), your mood, overall study time, and any external distractions.

The next stage is to conduct some kind of self test. Ideally, this will be a standardised test of some kind, such as a set of multiple choice questions from a practice exam. It may be easier, however, to prepare a set of flashcards at the end of the learning session, and later use these to test yourself.

One last thing that must be kept constant, given that you will be doing the study tasks at different times: you need to keep the delay between study and test the same. So if you are comparing this week's class with next week's, you will need to test yourself a week later, as well.

Other options

There are many other aspects of your study habits that you could investigate. The great thing about taking time to investigate these habits is that none of it is wasted—while you test out methods of study, you are also learning. What's more, over time you will develop more efficient strategies that work well in your context and classes, and therefore become a more effective student.

The following examples would all be worthwhile topics of investigation:

- The best way to write summaries of a book chapter or article. How many words should you write? Compare taking brief versus detailed notes, e.g. one index card versus two sides of A4 paper, during the same length of study session. Test your memory of the content a week later (set a timer/alarm for this so that you don't forget).

- The best amount of spacing for your material. The timescales and type of learning that you are attempting form a unique set of constraints. Using a set of around 40 flashcards, test yourself until you get all of the answers right three times, dropping each flashcard once you have done so. Then divide the cards randomly into two piles, and set them aside. Restudy one after a day, and one after two weeks. Finally, test yourself a month later. Again, use reminders on your phone to ensure that you don't forget about the restudy sessions. This can be tried repeatedly with different time scales.

- Compare ways of taking notes in class. For one week, take detailed notes of as much information as you can. The next week, assuming similar types of lessons, take much briefer notes such as the Cornell system (see Chapter 4). Test your recall of both sets of information after a delay, for example two weeks after the final class.

These are just the beginning—there are many other aspects of your study habits that can be tested.

Two general things are worth remembering. One is that many of the strategies discussed in this book are what researchers have called *desirable difficulties*—things that make it harder, but in a way that is beneficial. The benefit of investigating your own learning is that you find out whether things that feel harder or slower might actually be useful. Not every difficulty is beneficial, however! For example, a gap-fill task can be a useful form of active learning, but if a text is already difficult to understand, adding gaps may just make it confusing or ambiguous. This sort of difficulty is not likely to be helpful.

The second point is that when testing yourself, it's worth remembering the timescale. A number of studies (for example the Roediger & Karpicke research described in Chapter 5) have found one pattern of results after a short delay, but a completely different pattern after a longer delay. If in doubt, test yourself using time delays that are relevant to how long you need to remember information for your exam (it generally it won't involve recall after just a few minutes.)

Review questions

1. What needs to be kept constant if you compare two or more study or note-taking strategies?
2. How and when should you test yourself after comparing types of study activity?

11

Conclusion

The overall argument of this book is that there are great benefits to be gained from modifying your study strategies, to bring them in line with the evidence from the science of learning and memory. Don't stick to methods you used in the early years of school and don't rely on mindless repetition or highlighting. Instead, view learning and revision as skills which you can develop. Doing so won't just help you now, but will have advantages for your learning far into the future.

The book has explained how we form new memories, as well as the need to focus attention and avoid multi-tasking. It has looked at the benefits of active and deep (meaningful) processing, as well as the role of dual coding in long-term memory.

On a more practical level, we have seen that it is important to take good quality notes, but also to make sure that our note-taking habits are efficient and sustainable over the long term. I have recommended the benefits of using flashcards—which lend themselves to retrieval practice, spacing and interleaving—but also of using summaries and concept maps to establish a comprehensive overview of a topic or subtopic.

When preparing for the final exam, we have seen how a good schedule is important, and that shorter, focused study sessions with frequent short breaks may well have the best results. I have also recommended investigating many of these processes in your own learning, via mini experiment-style comparisons of how well you learn.

Overall, though, it will be clear that there is no magic bullet when it comes to learning. Many students fail to learn and apply effective study habits because they are tempted by options which seem easier in the here and now—preferring studying with friends to working alone, or re-reading to writing topic summaries, for example. Effective study does involve hard work, but it is also much more efficient and saves time over the long term, and can be very motivating, particularly when linked to your own interests. With simple but effective changes both in class and when revising, I strongly believe that you or any other student can achieve a top grade.

12

Answers to review questions

Chapter 2

1. Cramming can be effective over short timescales but leads to a lot of forgetting, and is therefore very inefficient over the longer term.
2. Re-reading after having understood a text is a form of overlearning, i.e. continuing to study once mastery has been achieved. Such strategies have a very limited long-term effect on learning.
3. Highlighting large sections of text does not make it better remembered, but highlighting can be an active study task by which you categorise different types of information. This is much more beneficial.

Chapter 3

1. Belief that revision involves storing information in short-term memory/that learning is mainly about repetition/that memories are separate files like on a computer hard

drive/etc.

2. Using two parts of working memory at the same time can be more demanding, but as long as neither task is especially novel or requires us to focus all of our attention on it, it is possible to multi-task. This contrasts with attempting two tasks that use the same part of working memory.

3. The two types of long-term memory are episodic memory (memory for events) and semantic memory (memory for facts and knowledge).

4. Gist/semantic memories are more resilient and detail memories forgotten sooner, and so memories for detail need to be revised sooner.

Chapter 4

1. One way to judge our note-taking habits is to consider whether they result in good quality notes while taking the minimum possible time, and freeing up attention for other classroom tasks.

2. A section for traditional notes, a section for questions and key points, and a section for a written summary.

3. Skimming is fast reading, taking about a third of the time it would take to read a text in detail. This makes further study faster and more effective.

4. The best format is one that facilitates self-testing, such as writing a definition, question or prompt on one side and an item or set of items on the other.

Chapter 5

1. After one week.
2. A visual image alone will be better remembered because we spontaneously think of the word when we see an image, and it is therefore dual coded.
3. More depth and detail in the description/more visual/self-reference.

Chapter 6

1. It suggests that we should wait i.e. have a delay before restudy.
2. To see the benefits of a delay before restudy, you have to first ensure mastery in the initial study session.
3. Interleaving is beneficial when concepts are similar and easily confused, so it's best to interleave flashcards within a particular topic or school subject, rather than mixing all of your flashcards together.

Chapter 7

1. Yes. Attention is the central part of working memory, and you cannot take in new information if you don't pay attention to it.
2. Doodling may be able to help tackle mind-wandering, but it should be avoided during visual topics and in your revision/self-study time.
3. Typically a 'pomodoro' study session lasts 25 minutes

followed by a five-minute break.

Chapter 8

1. Scenario questions aim to test transfer of knowledge to real situations.
2. Explain/Describe/Name/Analyse/Evaluate/Discuss/Predict etc. These indicate the type of information the question is looking for.
3. Mnemonics are primarily useful for prompting recall.
4. To help consolidate new memories/problem solving and creativity/repairing and replenishing the brain.

Chapter 10

1. As much as possible should be kept constant, but in particular, difficulty of the material, and conditions (e.g. noise and time of day) during both the study session and the test.
2. You can test yourself using a standard test/exam, or by preparing a set of flashcards specifically for this purpose. The amount of time between the study activities and the test must be kept constant for the activities you are comparing, and should be relevant to your context (i.e. not just using an immediate test).

Further information

Get more ideas about the science of learning and find out about Jonathan's other books and publications via his website, jonathanfirth.co.uk

Useful sites for creating online flashcards include Quizlet.com and studyblue.com, and their associated apps.

There are many good websites for further information about learning and revision, but also an even greater number of not-so-good ones! For an evidence-based site with a wide range of resources and blog posts aimed at students, I recommend the Learning Scientists website learningscientists.org. Retrieval Practice—retrievalpractice.org—is also very helpful and has a great newsletter, while The Emotional Learner—theemotionallearner.com—is excellent on the psychology of learning including motivation, emotion and personality.

A useful, detailed guide to taking Cornell notes (with illustrations) can be found at www.wikihow.com/Take-Cornell-Notes. Examples of concept maps can be viewed at jonathanfirth.co.uk/maps

Notes

INTRODUCTION

1 Yan, V.X., Bjork, E.L. and Bjork, R.A. (2016). On the difficulty of mending metacognitive illusions: A priori theories, fluency effects, and misattributions of the interleaving benefit. *Journal of Experimental Psychology: General,* 145(7): 918-33.

2 Hartwig, M. K., & Dunlosky, J. (2012). Study strategies of college students: Are self-testing and scheduling related to achievement?. *Psychonomic Bulletin & Review,* 19(1), 126-134

FLAWED STRATEGIES, AND WHY THEY ARE FAILING YOU

3 Kornell, N. (2009). Optimising learning using flashcards: Spacing is more effective than cramming. *Applied Cognitive Psychology,* 23, 1297–1317.

4 Metcalfe, J., & Kornell, N. (2005). A region of proximal learning model of study time allocation. *Journal of Memory and Language,* 52(4), 463-477.

5 Callender, A. A., & McDaniel, M. A. (2009). The limited benefits of rereading educational texts. *Contemporary Educational Psychology,* 34(1), 30-41.

6 Paivio, A., Rogers, T. B., & Smythe, P. C. (1968). Why are pictures easier to recall than words?. *Psychonomic Science,* 11(4), 137-138.

7 Yue, C. L., Storm, B. C., Kornell, N., & Bjork, E. L. (2015). Highlighting and its relation to distributed study and students' metacognitive beliefs. *Educational Psychology Review,* 27(1), 69-78.

WHAT IS LEARNING?

8 Bjork, R.A. (1975). Retrieval as a memory modifier. In R.L. Solso (Ed.) *Information Processing and Cognition: The Loyola symposium* (pp. 123–144). Hillsdale, NJ: Lawrence Erlbaum.

9 Piaget, J. (1952). *The Origins of Intelligence in Children* (M. Cook, trans). New York: International Universities Press.

10 https://dictionary.cambridge.org/dictionary/english/restaurant

11 Szpunar, K.K., Khan, N.Y. and Schacter, D.L. (2013). Interpolated memory tests reduce mind wandering and improve learning of online lectures. *PNAS* 110(16), 6313–6317.

12 Brainerd, C.J.; Reyna, V.F.; Kneer, R. (1995). False-recognition reversal: When is similarity distinctive?. *Journal of Memory and Language, 34*(2), 157–185.

STUDY HABITS

13 Adler, M. J., & Van Doren, C. (1940). *How to Read a Book* (Revised and Updated Edition). Simon and Schuster.

14 Blunt, J. R., & Karpicke, J. D. (2014). Learning with retrieval-based concept mapping. *Journal of Educational Psychology, 106*(3), 849.

MAKING THE LEARNING LAST

15 Roediger III, H. L., & Karpicke, J. D. (2006). Test-enhanced learning: Taking memory tests improves long-term retention. *Psychological Science, 17*(3), 249-255.

16 Bevan, W., & Steger, J. A. (1971). Free recall and abstractness of stimuli. *Science, 172*(3983), 597-599.

17 Paivio, A., & Csapo, K. (1973). Picture superiority in free recall: Imagery or dual coding?. *Cognitive Psychology, 5*(2), 176-206.

18 Zamary, A., Rawson, K. A., & Dunlosky, J. (2016). How accurately can students evaluate the quality of self-generated examples of declarative concepts? Not well, and feedback does not help. *Learning and Instruction, 46*, 12-20.

THE IMPORTANCE OF YOUR STUDY SCHEDULE

19 Vlach, H. A., Sandhofer, C. M., & Bjork, R. A. (2014). Equal spacing and expanding schedules in children's categorization and generalization. *Journal of Experimental Child Psychology, 123*, 129-137.

20 Cepeda, N. J., Vul, E., Rohrer, D., Wixted, J. T., & Pashler, H. (2008). Spacing effects in learning: A temporal ridgeline of optimal retention. *Psychological Science, 19*(11), 1095-1102.

21 Zulkiply, N., & Burt, J. S. (2013). The exemplar interleaving effect in inductive learning: Moderation by the difficulty of category discriminations. *Memory & Cognition, 41*(1), 16-27.

22 Carvalho, P. F., & Goldstone, R. L. (2014). Putting category learning in order: Category structure and temporal arrangement affect the benefit of interleaved over blocked study. *Memory & Cognition, 42*(3), 481-495.

23 Rohrer, D., Dedrick, R. F., & Stershic, S. (2015). Interleaved practice improves mathematics learning. *Journal of Educational Psychology, 107*(3), 900.

FOCUS AND PASSION

24 Baddeley, A. (2003). Working memory: looking back and looking forward. *Nature Reviews Neuroscience, 4*(10), 829-839.

25 Smallwood, J., & Schooler, J. W. (2006). The restless mind. *Psychological Bulletin, 132*(6), 946-958.

26 Andrade, J. (2010). What does doodling do?. *Applied Cognitive Psychology, 24*(1), 100-106.

27 Wammes, J. D., Meade, M. E., & Fernandes, M. A. (2016). The drawing effect: Evidence for reliable and robust memory benefits in free recall. *Quarterly Journal of Experimental Psychology, 69*(9), 1752-1776.

28 Fenesi, B., Lucibello, K., Kim, J. A., & Heisz, J. J. (2016). Sweat so you don't forget: How exercise breaks during instruction can promote learning. *Journal of Exercise, Movement, and Sport, 48*(1), 165.

29 Ceci, S. J., & Williams, W. M. (2010). Sex differences in math-intensive fields. *Current Directions in Psychological Science, 19*(5), 275-279.

EXAM PREPARATION

30 Wang, A. Y., Thomas, M. H., & Ouellette, J. A. (1992). Keyword mnemonic and retention of second-language vocabulary words. *Journal of Educational Psychology, 84*(4), 520-8.

JUST BEFORE YOUR EXAM

31 https://www.nytimes.com/2010/09/07/health/views/07mind.html

32 Woloshyn, V. E., Pressley, M., & Schneider, W. (1992). Elaborative-interrogation and prior-knowledge effects on learning of facts. *Journal of Educational Psychology, 84*(1), 115-124.

Index

Indexed material includes the content in chapters 1–11 including the introduction, and in addition the sections 'Answers to review questions' and 'Further information'. The preface and 'About the author' are not indexed.